T0054901

American Naval History: A Very Short Introduction

VERY SHORT INTRODUCTIONS are for anyone wanting a stimulating and accessible way into a new subject. They are written by experts, and have been translated into more than 45 different languages.

The series began in 1995, and now covers a wide variety of topics in every discipline. The VSI library now contains over 500 volumes—a Very Short Introduction to everything from Psychology and Philosophy of Science to American History and Relativity—and continues to grow in every subject area.

Very Short Introductions available now:

For more information visit our website

www.oup.com/vsi/

Craig L. Symonds

AMERICAN
NAVAL HISTORY

A Very Short Introduction

OXFORD
UNIVERSITY PRESS

OXFORD
UNIVERSITY PRESS

Oxford University Press is a department of the University of Oxford.
It furthers the University's objective of excellence in research, scholarship,
and education by publishing worldwide. Oxford is a registered trademark of
Oxford University Press in the UK and certain other countries.

Published in the United States of America by Oxford University Press
198 Madison Avenue, New York, NY 10016, United States of America.

© Oxford University Press 2016, 2018

Library of Congress Cataloging-in-Publication Data
Names: Symonds, Craig L., author.
Title: American naval history : a very short introduction / Craig L. Symonds.
Other titles: U.S. Navy.
Description: Oxford New York : Oxford University Press, [2018] |
Originally published: The U.S. Navy : a concise history, 2016. |
Includes bibliographical references and index.
Identifiers: LCCN 2017036028 (print) | LCCN 2017036317 (ebook) |
ISBN 9780199394784 (updf) | ISBN 9780199394791 (epub) |
ISBN 9780199394777 (online component) |
ISBN 9780199394760 (pbk. : alk. paper)
Subjects: LCSH: United States. Navy—History. |
CYAC: United States—History, Naval.
Classification: LCC E182 (ebook) | LCC E182 .S996 2018 (print) |
DDC 359.00973—dc23
LC record available at https://lccn.loc.gov/2017036028

1 3 5 7 9 8 6 4 2

Printed in Great Britain
by Ashford Colour Press Ltd., Gosport, Hants.
on acid-free paper

For Beatrice Witt Symonds

Contents

American Naval History

List of illustrations

Preface

In the second decade of the twenty-first century, the United States possesses the greatest navy on earth—it is not only more powerful than the navy of any other nation, it is arguably more powerful than all of them combined. It was not always so. In the early days of the Republic it was by no means certain that the country would have a navy at all. And even after the decision was made to create one, the national navy evolved in fits and starts along an uneven path. Its historical development from a handful of small sailing craft in the late eighteenth century to the juggernaut of today might best be understood as tracing a kind of sine wave— oscillating dramatically between periods of quiet torpor and moments of frenetic expansion. In pcacctime, a dedicated cadre of professionals operated and maintained a small permanent force that carried out the quotidian activities of a constabulary navy. Then, when roused by an emergency, the nation engaged in a frantic buildup to meet the crisis, after which the navy relapsed into its prewar character.

From the beginning, there were those who found this policy to be no policy at all. Champions of a large standing navy modeled on those of the great European powers, especially Britain, insisted that a formidable and visible American navy was an essential component of nationhood. To these navalists, a respectable navy was an important, even an essential, means of validating

America's nascent nationhood. Those not in sympathy with this view held that spending large sums of money to elicit foreign respect was the worst kind of fiscal profligacy. Even if the nation could afford it, they insisted, staking out a prominent place in the world was not a desirable goal, and they saw American participation in a global balance of power as both unnecessary and dangerous. Much of the early history of the U.S. Navy was characterized by a running dispute between these two views. Not until the mid-twentieth century, in the aftermath of two world wars, did the navalist view finally come to dominate.

This book is an account of the various peaks and troughs of that oscillating sine wave. It reviews the different missions assigned to the U.S. Navy in peacetime and the serial crises that led to its periodic expansion. Inevitably, it is also a story of changing technology as the Age of Sail gave way to the Age of Steam and Steel, to the Age of Carrier Warfare, and to our modern era of electronic and missile warfare. It is a story, too, of those who served, both on the quarterdeck and the forecastle, who took the navy in new or different directions or who served anonymously in a wide variety of roles ashore and afloat. This remarkable story, which so closely reflects the story of the United States itself, was punctuated by iconic moments of pure drama, and these, too, are part of the tale.

Chapter 1
An ad hoc navy: the Revolutionary War (1775–1783)

In the summer of 1775 the Massachusetts countryside around
Boston teemed with thousands of armed men, drawn there by
news that a column of British soldiers (redcoats or lobsterbacks,
in the dismissive vernacular) had opened fire on some militia
in the nearby village of Lexington in April, thus igniting the
American Revolution. Over the ensuing weeks and months
thousands of colonial militiamen arrived outside Boston, which
by midsummer was under a virtual siege. The city's peculiar
geography protected the British forces from a direct attack, for
in 1775 it was located on a peninsula that was connected to the
mainland only by a narrow isthmus, the Boston Neck. That
created a stalemate: the American militiamen could not fight their
way in, and the British could not fight their way out. Since the
only access to Boston was by water, and the Royal Navy
commanded the sea, the British remained secure and well
supplied inside the city no matter how many militiamen besieged
them. When a Virginian named George Washington arrived to
assume command of the colonial militia in the name of the
Continental Congress in July, he recognized that he had to find
a way to threaten the British supply line.

To do that Washington leased a fishing schooner, the *Hannah*, from
Colonel John Glover of Marblehead, Massachusetts, armed it with
four small cannon, and sent it to loot British ships. Thus the tiny

(78-ton) *Hannah* became the first armed vessel to act in the service of what would eventually become the United States of America.

The *Hannah*'s career as a warship was both short and disappointing. She captured only one vessel—which ironically turned out to belong to an American patriot—and not long afterward she ran aground and had to be abandoned. Soon enough, however, other vessels were entrusted with the same mission, and several of them made successful cruises, most notably the schooner *Lee*, which seized more than half a dozen British supply ships, including a Royal Navy ordnance brig loaded with 2,500 muskets, several cannon, and thirty tons of shot.

Washington's decision to employ armed vessels to sustain his siege of Boston proved a sound strategic gambit; before the siege was over, those vessels captured a total of fifty-five British ships. Significantly, however, the *Hannah*, the *Lee*, and the other ships of what came to be called Washington's navy were not part of a long-range plan to establish a permanent naval force. Rather they were an ad hoc response to particular circumstances, employed for a specific task in the full expectation that upon its completion they would revert to their former status as fishing schooners and merchant vessels. In that respect Washington's navy is a useful metaphor for the role of American naval forces in the Revolutionary War and indeed throughout much of the early history of the Republic.

Washington's siege of Boston ended in March 1776, after the Americans established artillery batteries on Dorchester Heights overlooking the city, and the British commander, William Howe, decided to abandon Boston and go to New York.

British naval dominance

The absence of an American naval force was painfully evident in Howe's swift occupation of New York City. Washington recognized from the outset that defending a city built on an island created daunting challenges for an army with no naval support, but he felt compelled to try. Howe's army very nearly trapped Washington's whole force, first on Long Island, then on Manhattan, and Howe might have destroyed the American army altogether if he had been more zealous. Instead Washington managed to escape, slipping away in the dark of the night to fight another day. The whole campaign, however, underscored the disadvantages of facing a foe that possessed unchallenged mastery of the sea.

In addition to scores of transport ships, Howe had brought to New York a fleet of ten ships of the line and twenty frigates, all under the command of his brother, Admiral Sir Richard Howe. Ships of the line, so called because they were powerful enough to hold a place in a naval line of battle, were the largest warships of the Age of Sail. Each of them carried seventy-four (or more) heavy naval guns arrayed on two decks, one above the other, and were therefore sometimes called two-deckers. Frigates had the same sail pattern as ships of the line (three masts, square rigged), but they were smaller and carried a single row of thirty-two to forty guns. Globally the Royal Navy boasted a total of 130 ships of the line and twice as many frigates. It was the largest navy in the world, and so dominant that Patriot forces could not hope to challenge it. Instead, like Washington at Boston, they employed such ersatz naval forces as they could when circumstances created an opportunity.

Lake Champlain

Champlain is a long and narrow lake that extends 125 miles from Lake George north of Albany, New York, to St. Johns in Quebec. In a country where roads were both few and poor, it was a vital north–south artery for travel and communication. In London British authorities contrived a scheme to send a military force southward from Canada along that artery to split rebellious New England off from New York and the middle colonies. It was evident from the outset of this campaign that whoever controlled Lake Champlain would command the strategic theater.

Once British intentions became evident, the Americans raced to augment the tiny squadron they had built on Lake Champlain. In a kind of miniature naval arms race, the British at the northern end and the Americans at the southern end each sought to conjure warships from the standing timber of the forests. The British took an early lead by disassembling an eighteen-gun sloop, the *Inflexible*, at Quebec and rafting sections of it up the St. Lawrence and Richelieu rivers to St. John, where it was reassembled. They also constructed two schooners and twenty gunboats, plus a giant raft-like vessel called a radeau, which they christened the *Thunderer*. Near Skenesboro, at the southern end of the lake, the Americans built six galleys with eight to ten guns each, plus six flat-bottomed, single-masted vessels called gundalows that carried three guns each. To command these vessels Washington dispatched the mercurial and energetic thirty-five-year-old Colonel Benedict Arnold.

The ensuing naval engagement on Lake Champlain, the Battle of Valcour Island, was a clear British victory. In an all-day fight on October 11, 1776, the American squadron was badly mauled. That night Arnold's surviving ships slipped past the British in the dark. The British gave chase, and one by one the American vessels were overtaken and driven ashore, their crews disappearing into the forest. While the British had secured control of the lake, the lengthy arms race, and the battle itself, had taken up most of the good summer and fall weather. With winter coming on, the British decided to wait until spring before continuing southward. That proved a fateful decision, for the long delay granted the Americans time to assemble an army that could contend with the British threat, and the result was an American victory a year later in the Battle of Saratoga. In hindsight it is evident that although Arnold lost the battle on Lake Champlain, he won a kind of strategic victory by making possible the American triumph at Saratoga.

Once again, however, Arnold's squadron was not part of an American commitment to creating a permanent naval force on

Lake Champlain or anywhere else. The men who fought on his galleys and gundalows were militia soldiers, not navy sailors. Though Skenesboro advertises itself to this day as the birthplace of the American navy, Arnold's little fleet, like Washington's navy, disappeared with the end of the campaign.

The Continental Navy

From the start a few Americans dreamed of creating a standing navy constructed on the British model. Their ambition was prompted less by a conviction that such a force might actually be able to contend with the mighty Royal Navy than from a belief that an American navy would confer legitimacy on American nationhood. The first hesitant steps toward the fulfillment of this vision can be traced back to October 13, 1775, when the Continental Congress in Philadelphia agreed to purchase two armed merchantmen to attack British supply ships, the first congressional appropriation of any kind for a maritime force. More significant, however, was a second resolution passed that same day establishing a standing committee to oversee the purchase of the ships and to write a set of regulations for their management. Thus was born the Continental Navy, and October 13 remains the official birth date of the U.S. Navy.

Two months later Congress took a more tangible step toward creating a navy by authorizing the construction of thirteen frigates, and a year later, in November 1776, Congress approved the construction of three ships of the line. This latter decision was stunningly ambitious. Ships of the line consumed prodigious amounts of seasoned timber and scores of heavy iron cannon and required a crew of between six hundred and eight hundred men. Frigates were much smaller, and the American decision to build thirteen of them was more realistic, but three ships of the line and a baker's dozen of frigates could hardly challenge the power of the Royal Navy, and the subsequent history of these ships provided the skeptics of a standing navy with powerful evidence of the perils of overreach.

To ensure the broadest public support for the frigate program, the building sites were scattered along the Atlantic seaboard. Warship construction was a lengthy process in the best of circumstances, and though the American colonists had built hundreds of merchant and fishing vessels, they had little experience building large warships or forging the kind of heavy naval guns they carried. The result was unanticipated delays and unforeseen expenses. Indeed while the ships at New York, Philadelphia, and Charleston, South Carolina, were still under construction, the British captured all three of these cities, and the unfinished ships had to be abandoned or burned.

The six frigates that were completed, fitted out, and manned were able to get to sea, but their record as warships was dismal, and it became evident almost at once that the entire program had been misguided. One of those ships, the *Warren*, was set afire by its own crew after it was chased ashore by a superior British force in Penobscot Bay, Maine (then part of Massachusetts). The other five were all captured or destroyed at sea. In many cases they were simply overwhelmed by larger and stronger ships, though they did not fare well even when they met a foe of comparable size and force. The most humiliating example of this was the case of the captured Continental Navy frigate *Hancock*. The British brought her into the Royal Navy as the *Isis*, and bearing that name she captured her own American sister ship, the *Trumbull*. The sad record of these thirteen frigates was so dispiriting that one of the champions of a standing American navy, John Adams, wrote to a friend that when he contemplated the history of the Continental Navy, it was hard for him to avoid tears.

John Paul Jones

The Continental Navy did have some moments of glory, many of them associated with the exploits of John Paul Jones. Born John Paul in 1747 in Scotland, Jones added his surname after fleeing to America in 1773 to avoid prosecution for killing a mutineer on the

West India merchantman *Betsy*. Jones cast his lot with the Patriot cause and won a commission as a lieutenant in the new Continental Navy. His initial duty was as the first lieutenant on the Continental Navy ship *Alfred* under the overall command of Commodore Esek Hopkins. In 1776 the Continental Congress ordered Hopkins to patrol the waters of the Chesapeake Bay and the Carolina coast. Instead Hopkins took his little squadron to the Bahamas, where he captured a small British fort and carried away some munitions, though otherwise contributed little to the war effort. More creditably Jones subsequently commanded the tiny twelve-gun sloop *Providence*, demonstrating both nautical skill and an aggressive temperament. In 1778 he carried news of the American victory at Saratoga to France in the sloop *Ranger*. Arriving in Quiberon Bay in February, the *Ranger* was greeted with a salute from the French fort on shore, the first international recognition of the American flag.

Jones was an ambitious man who burned to gain a reputation as a professional officer as well as a competent mariner. Though British newspapers routinely depicted him as a pirate for his seizure of British merchantmen, Jones hoped to put the lie to this characterization by challenging and defeating a ship of the Royal Navy. He fulfilled that ambition on April 24, 1778, when he defeated HMS *Drake* in a ship-to-ship duel in the Irish Sea. After that Jones sought a bigger ship, and eventually he received command of a former French East Indiaman, which the French government made available to him. Because the American ambassador to France, Benjamin Franklin, helped Jones obtain the ship, Jones christened it the *Bonhomme Richard*, a rough translation of "Poor Richard," in honor of Franklin's famous *Almanack*. It was in the *Bonhomme Richard* that Jones achieved his iconic victory and provided the Continental Navy with its signal achievement of the war.

On September 23, 1779, while in the North Sea off Flamborough Head with his own ship and several others, Jones intercepted a convoy of British ships from the Baltic. The convoy was escorted by two British warships, the brand-new oversize frigate *Serapis* and a smaller twenty-gun sloop. Jones immediately squared off against the *Serapis*, leaving the sloop and the convoy vessels to the other ships of his squadron. Early in the fight one of Jones's 18-pounder main deck guns burst upon firing, and rather than risk another such disaster, he continued the fight with only his weather-deck guns. As a result the *Bonhomme Richard* was badly mauled, and the commander of the *Serapis*, Richard Pearson, called across to ask Jones if he had surrendered. "Have you struck?" Pearson called out. To which Jones replied, "I have not yet begun to fight!"

1. From the deck of the captured British frigate *Serapis*, John Paul Jones salutes the *Bonhomme Richard* as it sinks in the North Sea after the Battle of Flamborough Head on September 23, 1779. At the height of that battle, the captain of the *Serapis* asked Jones if he had surrendered, to which Jones famously replied: "I have not yet begun to fight."

Eventually, when a fire on board the *Serapis* got out of control and threatened to ignite the ship's powder magazine, Pearson himself had to surrender. The Americans took possession of the *Serapis* and succeeded in putting out the fire, which was just as well since the battered *Bonhomme Richard* subsequently sank, and Jones had to transfer his crew to the British ship. Though this ship-to-ship victory, achieved literally within sight of the British coast, did little to change the course of the naval war, it provided a substantial boost to American morale.

Privateers

One aspect of naval warfare at which the Americans proved especially adept was commerce raiding. Not only did it strike at the British economy and thereby weaken public resolve, but it offered practitioners the possibility of making a fortune since the law of the sea held that captured ships and their cargoes became the property of the captors. Continental Navy ships seized merchant ships whenever they could, but the most effective commerce raiders during the Revolutionary War were scores of privately owned vessels known as privateers. Though often called pirates in the British press, privateers held government-issued letters of marque, which were quite literally licenses to steal. Such ships had been used effectively by the French against the British (and by Americans against the French) throughout the long series of Anglo-French wars that had begun back in 1689.

Obtaining a letter of marque was relatively easy. Though records are incomplete, somewhere between 1,700 and 2,000 American ship owners applied to Congress for one, though only about eight hundred American privateers actually got to sea. They ranged in size from tiny vessels hardly bigger than a ship's longboat to ship-rigged vessels with twenty guns or more. Some armed merchant ships obtained a letter of marque opportunistically hoping to meet a weaker British vessel. Others were dedicated privateers with oversize crews whose principal function was to seek out and attack British shipping. Before the war was over, American privateers captured an estimated six hundred British merchant ships and had a significant impact on the British economy, which contributed to British war weariness.

The disappointing performance of the Continental Navy and the success of commerce raiding led many Americans of the revolutionary generation to conclude that the job of defending American interests at sea could be done at no cost by hundreds of privateers. Many saw privateers as the militia of the sea: available in time of need yet requiring no public funds to sustain them in peacetime. In the years since, some naval historians have denigrated the impact of privateers, arguing that they used up naval stores and manpower that might otherwise have been committed to a standing navy. Yet given the limited naval assets of the colonies in the revolutionary era, commerce raiding was very likely the most effective maritime strategy within their reach.

The French navy

By far the most important naval engagement of the Revolutionary War involved no American ships at all. This was the Battle of the Capes, fought on September 5, 1781, near the mouth of the Chesapeake Bay. After the American success in the Battle of Saratoga in 1777, the French government signed a treaty with the upstart Americans as a way of exacting revenge on their British foes, who had bested them in the Seven Years War (1756–63). This turned the revolt of the American colonies into a global conflict. In the summer of 1781 the French sent a large fleet of ships of the line under Rear Admiral François J. P. Comte de Grasse from the Caribbean to the Chesapeake Bay to cooperate with a Franco-American army under Washington.

Washington knew that this was a priceless opportunity. Previously, whenever a British army found itself in difficulty, it marched to a nearby seaport, where it could be supplied, reinforced, or, if necessary, evacuated by the Royal Navy. Only when they strayed too far from the sea—as they had at Saratoga—did the British find themselves cut off from this succor. Thus in the fall of 1781, when Major General Charles Cornwallis, conducting an extended campaign through the Carolinas and Virginia, found himself in need of support, he headed for the small Virginia coastal town of Yorktown to rendezvous with the Royal Navy. The French Navy got there first. When British Rear Admiral Thomas Graves arrived from New York with his own fleet of ships of the line, the French fought his fleet to a tactical draw, and Graves returned to New York, leaving Cornwallis to his fate. Though the war straggled on for a few more years, the surrender of Cornwallis's army in October 1781 was decisive. The Peace of Paris was signed on September 3, 1783, and the United States became a nation.

The United States won its independence largely because the determination of the Patriot forces outlasted the British willingness to fight—and to pay for—a war three thousand miles away. Though, with the exception of John Paul Jones, the Continental Navy had proved mostly disappointing, the predations of American privateers had played a major role in eroding Parliamentary support for the war. Ersatz fleets at Boston and on Lake Champlain had played a role too, but it was American perseverance, personified by General George Washington, that was the principal contributor to victory. The surrender of Cornwallis at Yorktown, effected by the successful French defense of the Chesapeake Bay in the Battle of the Capes, was simply the final straw for Parliament, which had grown tired of a lengthy and costly conflict.

Chapter 2
Establishing an American navy: the Age of Sail (1783–1809)

With independence secured, the American militia returned to their farms, and privateersmen once again became merchant seamen. The few Continental Navy warships that had survived the conflict were sold off or given away; the last of them, the frigate *Alliance*, was auctioned off in 1785 and became a merchant ship on the China trade. Of the three ships of the line authorized nearly seven years earlier, only one had been completed before the war ended, and it never saw active service. Seeing no practical use for such a vessel in peacetime, Congress voted to give her to France both as a gesture of gratitude and to replace the French *Magnifique*, which had run aground coming into Boston Harbor in 1782. In effect the American navy simply ceased to exist. It was unclear in any case how the weak government created in 1781 under the Articles of Confederation could meet the expense of a peacetime navy given the impecunious state of the national treasury. Indeed it was the weakness of the national government, and in particular its inability to raise revenue, that led to the calling of a Constitutional Convention in Philadelphia in 1786.

The creation of a navy was not a major issue in Philadelphia, though it was occasionally cited as one reason a stronger central government was essential. The Constitution that emerged from the convention in 1787, which was eventually ratified by all thirteen states, stated only that Congress had the authority to "provide and maintain a navy" and to pass laws for its regulation. Whether Congress should actually do so, however, remained a matter of some dispute. Most Americans continued to conceive of a standing navy as both expensive and unnecessary. What dramatically changed that conversation was the emergence of a threat to American shipping in the Mediterranean.

The Barbary threat

The interminable Anglo-French conflict, which had worked decisively to America's advantage during the Revolution, proved troublesome after 1793, when British diplomats convinced Portugal to join an anti-French coalition. In order to have the means to do so, Portugal signed a peace treaty with the city-state of Algiers on the north coast of Africa and ended its regular patrols of the Straits of Gibraltar. Almost at once raiding ships from Algiers passed out into the Atlantic, where they began to attack American shipping.

The attacks provoked earnest discussion in Philadelphia about how to respond. It was evident that unleashing American privateers against the Algerines would have no effect at all, for the Barbary states had scant merchant trade for them to seize. What was needed was a national naval force that could both protect American commerce and punish those who attacked it. Appreciation of that reality led to a bill in Congress to authorize "a naval force, adequate to the protection of the commerce of the United States against the Algerine corsairs." Once again the idea was not to create a permanent naval establishment but to produce a temporary force to meet an immediate need. The specific proposal was for the construction of six large frigates, a decision that essentially founded the U.S. Navy, though only a few of those who supported the bill conceived of it in those terms. Most saw it as a short-term solution to an immediate problem, and to underscore that, Congress added a final section to the bill specifying that "if peace shall take place between the United States and the Regency of Algiers,…no further proceeding [shall] be had under this act."

The six frigates were noteworthy not only because they were the first warships approved by the new government but also because of their remarkable design. Larger and more stoutly built than conventional frigates, they were in effect frigates on steroids, capable of carrying as many as fifty or even sixty guns. The individual most responsible for this was Philadelphia shipbuilder Joshua Humphreys, who, along with his assistant Josiah Fox, drafted the plans for their construction.

Passing the legislation and drawing up the plans was the easy part. There were delays and unforeseen expenses in the construction process, and none of the ships had been completed when news arrived that American negotiators had concluded a treaty of peace with Algiers. Under its terms the United States would present Algiers with a thirty-six-gun frigate and pay $642,500, plus an additional annual payment of $21,600 in naval stores. In exchange Algiers would pledge not to attack American vessels. To modern eyes such terms are offensive—no better than simple extortion. But in 1795 paying extortion was the standard protocol for Western powers in dealing with the North African city-states. Pragmatists in the American Congress were perfectly willing to pay a reasonable tribute to Algiers, and to the other North African states as well, if it would secure the safety of American commerce, and they quickly ratified the treaty.

According to the stipulations of the 1794 act, work on the six frigates was now supposed to stop, but not everyone agreed that this was a good idea. Many congressmen, including some who supported the establishment of a permanent American navy, argued that it would be foolish and profligate to waste money already spent by stopping now. Besides, the Algerines might renege on their agreement, and it would be useful to have a few ships in readiness. In the end Congress agreed that three of the six frigates should be completed and that the president would have discretionary authority to complete the other three in the event of a new crisis.

The Quasi War

The new crisis turned out to have nothing at all to do with the Barbary corsairs. The French Revolution of 1789 turned the century-old Anglo-French conflict into an ideological struggle, and with the renewal of the war France invoked the mutual assistance clause in the Treaty of Paris, calling on the United States to join her. The Washington administration demurred. The official explanation was that the United States had concluded a treaty with the government of Louis XV and the obligation had lapsed when the monarchy ended. The real reason, of course, was that the United States simply did not want to get dragged into a European war.

This infuriated the French, who were angered further when the United States signed a trade agreement with Britain, known as Jay's Treaty, in 1795. The French responded by targeting American merchant ships that traded with British ports, especially in the Caribbean, where British and French colonies occupied alternating islands in the Lesser Antilles. Soon French warships (and ironically French privateers) began to seize American merchant vessels that were trading with the English. That led the new American president, John Adams, to send a three-man commission to France to negotiate a settlement. When that trio arrived in Paris, however, a representative of the French foreign minister requested a fee of $250,000 as a goodwill gesture before negotiations could begin. While this was business as usual in Europe, it provoked an uproar in America, where it became known as the XYZ Affair since the French emissaries were identified in the dispatches only as X, Y, and Z.

Though paying tribute to the dey of Algiers had raised few eyebrows in Congress, the notion of paying a bribe to French diplomats outraged congressmen. Rather disingenuously they cried, "Millions for defense, but not one cent for tribute," and in a rush passed several bills: one to complete and outfit all six of the frigates initially authorized four years earlier, another to approve the purchase of sixteen armed sloops, and a third to authorize American warships to attack French privateers in the Caribbean. Congress stopped short of declaring war on France, and the ensuing hostilities were confined to naval engagements in the Caribbean, circumstances that gave the conflict its historical name, the Quasi War (1798–1801).

Important as these measures were to the future of a U.S. Navy, a far more significant piece of legislation that summer resulted from the perceived need to create a central authority to superintend all these ships, a "Commissioner of Marine," as it was initially called. To do that, in May 1798 Congress authorized the creation of a Department of the Navy, and in June President Adams appointed Maryland merchant Benjamin Franklin Stoddert as the nation's first secretary of the navy. That summer Congress also passed An Act for the Relief of Sick and Disabled Seamen, which provided healthcare paid for by a mandatory tax on sailors. The establishment of a Navy Department was decisive, in part because it created a center of advocacy for continued naval expansion.

The advocacy began almost at once. In December 1798, with the Quasi War in full flood, Stoddert urged Congress to approve the construction of twelve ships of the line, twelve frigates, and "twenty to thirty" smaller vessels. Since it would take years to complete such a project, it was evident that Stoddert's goal was not to obtain ships for use in the ongoing naval war with France but rather for a standing U.S. Navy. Such a proposal would have been unthinkable only a decade before, but early successes in the war with France created a climate in which it received serious consideration.

In fact American warships performed quite well against the French, particularly the frigate USS *Constellation* commanded by

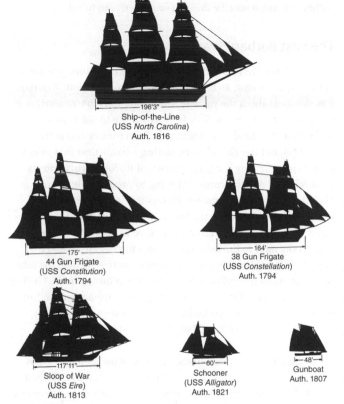

Ship-of-the-Line
(USS *North Carolina*)
Auth. 1816
196'3"

44 Gun Frigate
(USS *Constitution*)
Auth. 1794
175'

38 Gun Frigate
(USS *Constellation*)
Auth. 1794
164'

Sloop of War
(USS *Eire*)
Auth. 1813
117'11"

Schooner
(USS *Alligator*)
Auth. 1821
60'

Gunboat
Auth. 1807
48'

2. **Relative sizes of U.S. Navy warships in the Age of Sail**

Commodore Thomas Truxtun. In February 1799 Truxtun and the *Constellation* defeated the French frigate *L'Insurgente* in a spectacular ship-to-ship duel. That, and news of other victories, helped convince Congress to give Stoddert at least some of what he wanted, and the Naval Act of 1799 authorized funding for six ships of the line and six sloops. Even this half a loaf was an important victory for those who espoused a standing navy, for it was the first time the nation appropriated monies for warships without having a specific mission or objective in mind.

The First Barbary War

One year later Thomas Jefferson was elected the third president of the United States. A champion of small government, Jefferson was skeptical about the value of a standing navy, particularly one composed of ships of the line. He was willing to use frigates and sloops to defend American trade from pirates and petty potentates, but the idea of constructing a battle fleet that might take its place among the great powers of Europe struck him as both wasteful and dangerous. Hoping to preempt him from abolishing the navy altogether, Federalists in the lame duck Congress rushed through the Peace Establishment Act before Jefferson took office in March 1801. Specifically the new law limited the navy to thirteen frigates and further stipulated that only six of the thirteen were to be kept on active service; the others were to remain in readiness in the event of a future crisis. The U.S. Navy was thus confirmed as a standing peacetime organization even if half of it was to be laid up in ordinary—what a later generation would call "mothballs"—to await a crisis.

Meanwhile Jefferson made immediate use of the six frigates that remained on active service. He sent three of them, plus a sloop, to the Mediterranean, where the Barbary corsairs continued to pose a latent threat, and planned to rotate those ships with the other three frigates every six months to maintain a constant American presence in the Mediterranean. Jefferson called it a "squadron of observation."

The first such squadron, commanded by Commodore Richard Dale, who had served aboard the *Bonhomme Richard* with John Paul Jones, arrived in the Mediterranean in July 1801. There Dale learned that the bashaw of Tripoli, Yusuf Karamanli, had abrogated the existing treaty with the United States and declared war on American shipping. Unhappy with the $56,000 he had received for signing a treaty, Karamanli wanted something closer to the $642,000 the United States had paid to Algiers. From the moment he arrived, therefore, Dale found that he was responsible for conducting a war against Tripoli.

The war did not go well. Dale seemed unsure of what to do or how to do it, and his successor, Richard Valentine Morris, proved little better. Not until 1803, when Commodore Edward Preble arrived, did the American squadron in the Mediterranean have a commander who proved willing and able to prosecute the war vigorously. Preble established a close blockade of Tripoli and conducted periodic raids into the harbor. The most daring of these was led by Lieutenant Stephen Decatur, who sailed into Tripoli Harbor and burned the captured frigate *Philadelphia* without suffering the loss of a man. Congress subsequently rewarded Decatur for his audacious feat by promoting him to the rank of captain at the age of only twenty-five, still the youngest American ever to hold that rank.

The United States also opened a second front in the war by encouraging Karamanli's brother Hamet to challenge Yusuf as bashaw. During the Age of Sail each American warship carried a small contingent of marines whose mission was to maintain order aboard ship as the captain's constabulary, though they were occasionally used in shore expeditions. In 1801 eight U.S. Marines from Preble's squadron joined a ragtag Arab army with Hamet at its head for an overland march on Tripoli from the east. That threat encouraged Yusuf to come to terms. For $60,000 he agreed to release all the American prisoners he had taken from the captured *Philadelphia* and to end the annual tributes. It did not end the tribute system altogether, but it demonstrated that there were limits to what the United States would tolerate.

Jefferson and the embargo

If the tiny U.S. Navy proved sufficient to bring Yusuf Karamanli to terms, it remained a negligible token in the interminable war between England and France. As far as Jefferson was concerned, that was just as well. The president was determined to stay out of the European war, and he quickly approved the Treaty of Mortefontaine that ended the Quasi War in July 1801. Jefferson was equally determined to avoid conflict with Britain. He knew that Britain's very survival hinged on her control of the sea and that any effort to challenge that control, even inferentially, could provoke a devastating preemptive strike. As if to demonstrate that, in April 1801 Britain attacked and virtually annihilated the battle fleet of neutral Denmark simply for declaring its intention to protect its own shipping. Unwilling to attract similar hostile attention from the Royal Navy, and hopeful that the broad Atlantic would keep America insulated from the seemingly endless war in Europe, Jefferson consistently opposed any effort to build an American fleet of ships of the line.

American hopes of staying uninvolved were threatened by the historic events of 1805. In that pivotal year the British naval victory over a Franco-Spanish fleet at Trafalgar in October and the French victory over the combined armies of Russia and Austria at Austerlitz in December made each of the rivals supreme in its own element: Britain ruled the waves, and Napoleon ruled the continent. Unable to come directly to grips with one another, each side sought to weaken its foe through economic sanctions. The United States was caught in the middle.

At first the sanctions had little impact on the United States. Napoleon lacked the naval power to enforce his pronouncements, especially after Trafalgar, and since Britain was America's principal trading partner anyway, business mostly went on as usual. Gradually, however, the sanctions became more annoying, and soon other factors contributed to an erosion of Anglo-American relations. One was the Royal Navy's desperate need for men. In order to maintain its blockade of continental France and to patrol the sea lanes of the world, the Royal Navy's appetite for manpower was insatiable. Occasionally, and then increasingly, Royal Navy ships began taking sailors off American merchant ships they met at sea, especially when the men were—or were thought to be—English citizens or, worse, deserters from the Royal Navy.

A particularly divisive event took place in the summer of 1807 off the Virginia capes when the captain of the fifty-gun HMS *Leopard* signaled the thirty-eight-gun frigate USS *Chesapeake* that he was sending over a boat. The American commodore James Barron assumed that the British warship had dispatches for him and hove to. Instead a British officer came on board the *Chesapeake* with a demand that four members of the *Chesapeake*'s crew, believed to be Royal Navy deserters, must be given up. When Barron refused, the *Leopard* opened fire, unleashing seven unanswered broadsides into the *Chesapeake* before Barron finally managed to fire a single gun and then struck his flag. The British recovered their deserters, and the battered American frigate limped back into port. Barron was court-martialed for being unprepared, but the more important question was how the United States should respond to this flagrant insult. It might have meant war, but instead Jefferson opted for economic sanctions of his own, closing American ports to British warships and declaring a trade embargo, effectively forbidding Americans to trade with any other nation.

Jefferson's embargo policy pleased almost no one. American merchants, especially those in New England, were particularly angered, and they routinely violated the restrictions just as they had ignored the trade regulations imposed on them by the British Parliament during the colonial era. The small U.S. Navy found itself in the unhappy role of enforcing the embargo, assuming duties uncomfortably similar to those that had been exercised by the Royal Navy a generation earlier. To some New Englanders the U.S. Navy had become the enemy.

The gunboat navy

Even if the embargo succeeded in keeping American vessels beyond the reach of the British, there was still the issue of how the United States could defend the sovereignty of its own harbors. To do that Jefferson opted for the construction of scores of small gunboats, much like those Preble had used so successfully during the war against Tripoli.

Compared to ships of the line, or even to frigates, gunboats were tiny; most were only sixty to eighty feet long and had only a single mast and often only a single gun, generally a 24- or 32-pounder. They were also inexpensive; at roughly $5,000 each, more than two dozen of them could be had for the price of a single frigate. They were also strictly defensive weapons and therefore unlikely to provoke a confrontation with Britain. They appealed to the advocates of a militia-based naval force because when they were not in active service, they could be laid up in large sheds or barns. Like the soldier's musket on the mantelpiece, they could be kept near to hand in case of an emergency but did not require extensive maintenance.

During Jefferson's second term (1805–9) the United States built more than a hundred of these gunboats, boasting a total of 172 of them by the late summer of 1809. Fifty-four of them were concentrated in New York Harbor; twenty-one more were based in Norfolk to defend the Chesapeake Bay; and twenty-four operated out of New Orleans to defend the Mississippi River. Philadelphia, Charleston, and Baltimore each had smaller squadrons.

Champions of a traditional navy on the European model despised the gunboat program and argued that the money poured into it would have been better spent on oceangoing warships that could establish a foundation for a future U.S. Navy. There is no way to know what might have ensued had Jefferson opted for a frigate navy, even assuming that a budget-conscious Congress would have approved such a thing. By building a gunboat navy, Jefferson provided a veneer of defense for the coast without sailing into the dangerous waters of the Anglo-French conflict.

Chapter 3
An American navy confirmed:
the War of 1812

In May 1811 Royal Navy Captain Samuel Pechell, commander of the British thirty-eight-gun frigate HMS *Guerriére*, stopped an American merchant ship off Sandy Hook within sight of the New Jersey shore. After a brief search by a boarding party, the British removed an American sailor, one John Diggo of Maine, brought him on board the *Guerriére*, and absorbed him into the crew. Royal Navy ships had been pressing American sailors into service for years, but this was a particularly high-handed example, and when word of it reached U.S. Navy Captain John Rodgers, commanding the forty-four-gun frigate *President*, he set out in pursuit. Off the Virginia Capes, Rodgers espied a vessel rigged as a warship and, assuming her to be the *Guerriére*, gave chase. That night, just past 10:00, he was close enough to demand that the vessel identify herself. When he received no satisfactory reply, he opened fire, though he later insisted that the other ship fired first. The heavy guns of the *President* soon overwhelmed the other vessel, which the coming of dawn revealed to be not the *Guerriére* but the now terribly battered twenty-two-gun sloop HMS *Little Belt*. Rodgers offered to send over a party of sailors to help make repairs, but the offer was declined, and the *Little Belt*, with nine killed and twenty-three wounded, limped off to Halifax to refit. Some Americans thought it was a suitable revenge for the attack by HMS *Leopard* on the *Chesapeake* four years earlier.

The road to war

In addition to the running sore of British impressment of American seamen, another grievance was British encouragement of the western Indians who occasionally raided settlements in the Old Northwest, especially in the Ohio and Indiana territories. A group of congressmen, mostly from the West and South, dubbed the Warhawks, were convinced that the best way to secure the Northwest Territory for the United States was to seize Canada. Ever since Colonel Benedict Arnold had led an expedition to Quebec in 1776, many Americans had conceived of Canada as a natural part of the United States. Because Britain was fully preoccupied by the continuing war with Napoleonic France, Canada was all but undefended, and the Warhawks believed that the fruit was ripe for picking.

Given the momentum toward war, it seemed to many in the Congress, and in the country at large, that it would be prudent to make some preparation for it and, in particular, to augment the small U.S. Navy. The Warhawks disagreed because they did not believe that expanding the navy would contribute to their goal of seizing Canada. Meanwhile most of those in Congress who did advocate a naval expansion opposed going to war at all. As a result of these divisions, even as the nation moved closer to war in the spring of 1812, Congress rejected a series of proposals to enlarge the navy. On June 1 President James Madison sent a war message to Congress, and two weeks later Congress voted for war. The day before the final vote, three thousand miles away in London, the British foreign secretary reported to the House of Commons that Britain was suspending its sanctions against the United States. It was too late. News of the British concession did not reach the United States for weeks, and by then the momentum of events was unstoppable.

Early campaigns

The American invasion of Canada bogged down almost at once. An American thrust toward Montreal fizzled when the New York

State militia refused to cross the border on the grounds that their duty did not extend beyond state lines. Another American army, under Major General William Hull, successfully crossed the Detroit River into Upper Canada, but almost at once Hull became concerned about his supply line and decided to retreat back to Fort Detroit. A small British army and its Indian allies pursued him there, and, fearful that his supply lines would be cut, Hull surrendered. Instead of an American invasion of Canada, the British now threatened to march into Ohio.

Nor was the early news from the navy particularly encouraging. There had been some discussion before hostilities began about the best way to deploy America's scarce naval assets. Most U.S. Navy ship captains hoped to conduct independent cruises against British commerce. That would not only allow them to cover the widest possible area, making the seas dangerous for British shipping; it would also create the best opportunity for them to secure prize money. Instead Captain Rodgers lobbied successfully for concentrating much of America's naval power into one squadron, which he, as the senior U.S. Navy officer at the time, would command.

Rodgers's squadron of three frigates and two sloops put to sea as soon as news of the American declaration of war reached New York. Rodgers hoped to catch and decimate a convoy of British ships from Jamaica before the Royal Navy learned that war had been declared. Off New York Rodgers and his five ships encountered a lone British frigate, the HMS *Belvidera*, and set out in pursuit. Though the *Belvidera*'s captain had no knowledge of the onset of hostilities, the sight of five U.S. warships bearing down led him to make the judicious decision to flee. Rodgers pursued, but unable to catch her, he then resumed his unsuccessful search for the Jamaica convoy.

After eleven weeks at sea Rodgers returned to Boston on the last day of August 1812, with little to show for his efforts. He maintained in his report that the very existence of his squadron abroad in the Atlantic had played an important strategic role by forcing the British to concentrate their naval forces there as well. The claim had some merit, for the British did withdraw forces from the American coast in order to convoy British merchant ships, which very likely protected American merchant ships as they returned to port. Nevertheless the absence of any more tangible accomplishment by Rodgers's squadron led to a reassessment of how best to use the handful of American frigates. Abandoning the effort to concentrate its meager forces, the United States decided instead to scatter them across the seas. That led to a number of individual ship-to-ship engagements between American and British frigates that greatly boosted American morale.

The frigate duels

The first such engagement took place on August 19, 1812, when the forty-four-gun USS *Constitution* under Captain Isaac Hull (brother of the disgraced William Hull, who had surrendered Detroit) met the hated *Guerriére*, now commanded by twenty-four-year-old James Dacres, who would eventually become a British vice admiral.

Dacres handled his ship with skill, twice crossing the bows of the *Constitution*, but the battle became a slugfest when the two ships came together. The British generally won such encounters because their superbly trained gun crews could usually fire three broadsides to an enemy's two. In this case, however, the far heavier throw weight of the *Constitution*'s 24-pounder main battery soon reduced the *Guerriére* to a wreck. Moreover the thick oak sides of the *Constitution* proved remarkably resistant to the lighter weight of the British shot. When early ranging shots from the *Guerriére* bounced off her side, a crewman on the British frigate is supposed to have exclaimed, "By God, she's made of iron!," a remark that gave the *Constitution* her immortal nickname, "Old Ironsides." When Hull brought the *Constitution* back into Boston with the news of his victory, the American public went wild with joy.

Two months later Stephen Decatur in the frigate *United States* captured the British frigate *Macedonian*, and two months after that, in December, Commodore William Bainbridge, in command of the *Constitution*, met and defeated HMS *Java*, a relatively new British frigate that carried forty-six guns.

This trio of ship-to-ship victories could not be explained away solely by the superior broadside throw weight of the oversized American frigates, for during these same months the twenty-two-gun sloop USS *Wasp* defeated the similarly armed HMS *Frolic* in a single-ship encounter in October, and the following February the sloop USS *Hornet* defeated HMS *Peacock*. There were a few defeats for the fledgling U.S. Navy too, though each of those losses was to greatly superior force, and news of them did not deflate American giddiness about the early success of its warships. Gratifying as they were, these single-ship victories did little to affect the course of the war, and soon enough the American frigates found it difficult to get to sea at all once the British initiated a blockade of the ports where they were based.

In June 1813 Captain Philip Broke, commanding the frigate HMS *Shannon* off Boston, sent away the other British blockading ships and dispatched a note to Captain James Lawrence, who commanded the USS *Chesapeake* inside the harbor, "to try the fortune of our respective flags." Even before he received that note Lawrence prepared to go to sea, accepting the implied challenge of the *Shannon*'s lone presence off the harbor. More so than in the earlier frigate engagements, these two ships were evenly matched in terms of broadside throw weight, and the result was a frightful gun duel with very heavy losses—more than 220 combined casualties. With the ships close alongside, each sought to board the other, and Lawrence himself was mortally wounded trying to repel a British boarding party. His dying words were an order to his first lieutenant: "Don't give up the ship." The phrase became famous, but the *Chesapeake* was taken nonetheless, ending the drought of frigate victories for the Royal Navy.

The last frigate duel of the war was also an American defeat. In January 1815 Stephen Decatur, now in command of the USS *President,* tried to escape from New York Harbor in a blizzard. In the dark and amid the fury of the storm, he briefly ran aground, which slowed his passage, and the British blockading squadron spotted him. A long chase ensued, and after many hours HMS *Endymion* got close enough to open fire. Decatur might have been able to defeat *Endymion* in a single-ship engagement, but three more British frigates arrived, and Decatur had to strike his colors. The war ended soon afterward.

Other naval operations

Though the frigate duels commanded public attention, the American privateers once again played an important role, as they had during the American Revolution. More than five hundred eager American entrepreneurs obtained letters of marque from the Madison administration, and their ships ranged over much of the Atlantic, including the waters around England and Ireland, where British merchant ships seldom bothered with convoys or escorts. American privateers captured more than three hundred British merchant ships and burned many more. Maritime insurance rates, generally pegged at 1 percent or less of the value of the cargo, skyrocketed. Insurance companies charged British ships bound from Liverpool to Halifax as much as 30 percent of the value of their cargo to ensure its safe arrival, and that made it hard for shippers to make a profit even if they successfully managed to elude the privateers.

Along the American coast the swarm of American gunboats proved no match for the British warships. In June 1814 American Commodore Joshua Barney did the best he could with his small gunboat squadron in the Battle of St. Leonard's Creek, a tributary of the Chesapeake, but he could not stop the British from landing an army and marching on Washington, where they burned the government buildings in retaliation for similar American treatment of York in Upper Canada. Nor did the gunboats on Lake Borgne near New Orleans succeed in preventing a British force from landing near that city. The disappointing performance of the gunboats, especially when compared to the success of the frigates on the high seas, discredited the idea of relying on them for the nation's maritime defense.

The most strategically significant contribution of the navy during the war was a pair of battles that took place on freshwater lakes along the northern frontier. The first of these occurred on Lake Erie, where Master Commandant Oliver Hazard Perry defeated a British squadron under Captain Robert H. Barclay. Both Barclay and Perry faced crippling challenges in building, manning, and equipping their ships. The vessels themselves had to be built from standing timber, and the men who manned them were mostly militia soldiers, many of whom were, in the words of one of Perry's volunteers, "in totle ignorance of the servis." That volunteer also expressed his dismay that navy rations consisted of bread that was "mouldy & unfit for men to eat" and beef that was "putrid and covered with vermine."

In spite of these challenges, on September 10, 1813, Perry's small squadron met and defeated Barclay's squadron near Put in Bay, capturing every one of Barclay's ships. In a tribute to his friend James Lawrence, Perry flew a flag during the battle that was emblazoned with Lawrence's last words: "DONT GIVE UP THE SHIP." Moreover he added a line of his own to American naval lore by sending a quick note afterward to William Henry Harrison, the American army commander on shore: "We have met the enemy and they are ours."

Almost exactly one year later, on September 11, 1814, Master Commandant Thomas Macdonough accomplished a similar feat on Lake Champlain with equally important strategic results. Macdonough's victory over a British squadron under Captain John Downie near the location of the 1776 Battle of Valcour Island

3. Master Commandant Oliver Hazard Perry is rowed from the badly damaged USS *Lawrence* to the USS *Niagara* during the Battle of Lake Erie on September 10, 1813. The *Niagara* had remained out of the battle to this point, but Perry maneuvered her into the thick of the fight and emerged triumphant.

halted a British invasion effort and forced the British to retreat to Canada. These victories on Lake Erie and Lake Champlain had a strategic significance far greater than the modest size of the squadrons that engaged in them. Though the Warhawks' dream of seizing Canada had proved a folly, the victories of two small freshwater squadrons salvaged what might otherwise have been a disastrous campaign along America's northern border.

Peace

The defeat of Napoleon, first in the Battle of Nations at Leipzig in 1814, which led to his initial exile to Elba, and then definitively at Waterloo in 1815, finally ended the European war, and also ended the need for the Royal Navy to continue the impressment of American sailors. Already in 1814 British and American delegates were meeting in the city of Ghent, Belgium, to discuss an end to their war. Though there was some sentiment to make the Americans pay for what many Britons believed was treachery, the war with France had been going on for as long as anyone could remember, and most Britons were tired. The Treaty of Ghent was signed on Christmas Eve in 1814, though news of it did not reach the United States for more than a month.

In the meantime an American army commanded by Andrew Jackson defeated a British army under Edward Packenham south of New Orleans on January 8, 1815. News of that victory reached Washington at about the same time as news of the agreement in Ghent, and that encouraged a general impression that the United States had somehow won the war. Indeed many Americans concluded that the War of 1812 ratified the nation's sovereignty, and it became common to refer to it as the Second War for American Independence.

Public and congressional enthusiasm for the navy, already high, increased even more in the first few months of peace, when a squadron under Decatur returned from the Mediterranean to report another success. During the war with Britain the dey of Algiers had resumed his war on American commerce. Within days of the news from Ghent, therefore, Madison dispatched two separate American squadrons to the Mediterranean. Decatur commanded the first of them and, determined to redeem himself after his loss of the USS *President* to the *Endymion* a few months earlier, raced to the Mediterranean, captured the Algerine flagship, and appeared off Algiers itself to demand the dey's acceptance of a new treaty.

By 1816, therefore, Americans took great satisfaction from the fact that the navy had not only provided the most cheering news during the war with Britain but had also proved its utility in peacetime by suppressing Algiers. That fed enthusiasm for two pieces of postwar legislation. One, in 1815, established the Board of Navy Commissioners to supervise the navy and make plans for its employment. The other was An Act for the General Increase of the Navy, passed in April 1816, that appropriated $10 million over ten years in order to construct nine ships of the line "of not less than 74 guns each" plus twelve forty-four-gun frigates. As with the Humphreys-designed frigates authorized in 1794, each of the ships of the line was to be larger and more robustly armed than conventional vessels of their nominal class. Though rated as seventy-four-gun ships, they were designed to carry eighty or ninety guns, and one of them, the USS *Pennsylvania*, carried 120 guns, making it one of the most powerful warships afloat. As one supporter of the new legislation declared after its passage, this act "finally fixed and settled" the navy's status as a permanent branch of the government.

Another manifestation of the public acceptance of the navy was legislation in 1817 that for the first time established naval uniforms for enlisted men as well as officers. In summer the men were to wear uniforms of white duck, and in winter they would wear blue wool jackets, a circumstance that led to their nickname as "bluejackets."

Chapter 4

A constabulary navy: pirates, slavers, and manifest destiny (1820–1850)

The American ships of the line authorized in 1816 never fired a shot in anger. Though a few of them were dispatched one at a time to cruise the Mediterranean, they were afterward mostly laid up in ordinary. The kinds of tasks assigned to the U.S. Navy after 1820 were simply inappropriate for such huge—and expensive to operate—warships. The day-to-day duties of the U.S. Navy involved dealing with smugglers, pirates, and the illegal slave trade, and deploying ships of the line to deal with such issues was like hitting a tack with a sledgehammer. In addition the crumbling economy during the Panic of 1819 made the continued expenditure of $1 million a year for ships of the line seem foolish. The successful completion of treaties with both England and Spain demilitarized the Great Lakes and stabilized the country's southern border, which eased concerns about a future foreign war, and the petition of the Missouri Territory for admission to the Union as a slave state that same year turned the attention of the country inward to the West rather than outward toward the sea.

As a result of all these factors, in 1821 Congress halved the annual appropriation for the big ships of the line and committed the money thus saved to the construction of sloops and even smaller schooners. That same year Congress also passed legislation to construct large covered sheds where the ships of the line and frigates, stripped of their masts and rigging, could be housed.

Though the navy was permanently established, U.S. policy continued to reflect a Jeffersonian view that the big ships should be held in reserve as a kind of militia navy, while the daily activities of a peacetime navy were carried out by small squadrons of sloops and schooners acting as a constabulary force on distant stations abroad.

The first and foremost of these overseas stations was in the Mediterranean. While the Barbary peril had been all but eliminated by 1830, the United States continued to maintain a Mediterranean squadron, though its role became more ornamental than functional. One by one the big new ships of the line made their debut as flagships of the American Mediterranean squadron, and when combined with two or three frigates plus an equal number of sloops, the U.S. Navy could make quite a show. Using Port Mahon in Spanish Minorca as their base, the ships of the squadron cruised the periphery of the Mediterranean from Suez to Gibraltar. At each stop the local authorities were likely to host a dinner or a ball to honor the officers of the squadron while the sailors enjoyed shore leave in the way of sailors everywhere. As one officer recalled, orders to the Mediterranean were much like an invitation to "a perpetual yachting party." Other, much smaller squadrons operated in the West Indies, off Africa, in the Pacific, off Brazil, and in the East Indies to protect American trade and act as a kind of diplomatic presence to oversee U.S. interests abroad.

Pirates

The greatest threat to American trade continued to be from pirates, now in the Caribbean rather than the Mediterranean. Pirates had always been a concern in the West Indies, but their numbers increased dramatically during the 1820s due to special circumstances. Beginning in 1810 several of Spain's unhappy colonies in Central and South America initiated efforts to win their independence via wars of liberation. These revolutionary governments were generous in passing out letters of marque to prey on Spanish trade. Operating mostly in tiny single-masted cutters and schooners—even the occasional rowboat—these privateers found slim pickings in targeting Spanish vessels, and they soon began to seize any merchant ship they could catch. By 1820 most of them had metamorphosed from licensed privateering into open piracy, and in 1822 the U.S. Navy established the West Indies Squadron to deal with them.

The first commander of that squadron was Commodore James Biddle, who established his headquarters at Key West, Florida. Biddle found that the four big frigates assigned to him were all but useless against the small, shallow-draft pirate vessels, and it became evident that the task of combating the pirates could be accomplished more effectively and more cheaply by smaller and handier schooners and sloops, often operating independently.

The young lieutenants who commanded the ships of this "mosquito navy," as it was sometimes called, were endowed with broad responsibilities. Since it could take months to communicate with the government in Washington, or even with their commodore at Key West, they often had to make decisions on their own based on the circumstances of the moment. In September 1822 Lieutenant Stephen Cassin, commanding the sloop *Peacock*, discovered five pirate vessels taking shelter at Bahia Honda on the north coast of Spanish Cuba. He captured all five of the pirate vessels and then destroyed the settlement that had sheltered them even though it was in Spanish territory. Six months later, in the spring of 1823, Lieutenant Cornelius Stribling also attacked pirate vessels in Cuban waters not far from Havana, landing a shore party to pursue them when they fled inland. And three months after that two U.S. Navy schooners shelled a pirate fort on the south coast of Cuba, landing a shore party under twenty-two-year-old Lieutenant David Glasgow Farragut to complete the destruction. The Navy Department subsequently approved and even applauded all of these actions.

There were limits to what a U.S. Navy officer might do, however. In 1824 Captain David Porter, who had replaced Biddle as commander of the West Indian Squadron, sent two officers ashore in Spanish Puerto Rico to investigate whether the pirates were using the town of Fajardo to house some of their captured booty. The two officers wore civilian clothes, and Spanish authorities, suspicious of their activities, detained them, though only for a day. Nevertheless Porter believed this was an intolerable discourtesy, and he responded by landing two hundred sailors and marines, taking possession of the town, and threatening to destroy it if the Spanish did not issue a formal apology. Porter got his apology, but upon his return to the United States the next year he was court-martialed and suspended from duty for six months for exceeding his orders. To Porter this was an insult to his honor, and he resigned his commission, later accepting an admiral's commission from the government of Mexico. This episode reflected the fact that what naval officers in the Age of Sail called "honor" was often a kind of personal touchiness that led to both duels at home and international incidents abroad.

Pirates were a problem in other parts of the world too. One trouble spot was in the Far East, especially in the much-traveled Straits of Malacca between Malaya and Sumatra. In 1831 three boatloads of armed natives attacked the American merchantman *Friendship* near the village of Quallah Battoo on Sumatra (now Kuala Batu in Indonesia). The crew of the *Friendship* successfully fought off the pirates, but three of their number were killed in the struggle. President Andrew Jackson had a low threshold of tolerance for what he perceived to be insults to the national honor, and when he learned of the attack on the *Friendship*, he ordered the frigate USS *Potomac* to "chastise" the guilty parties. The *Potomac*, commanded by Commodore John Downes, arrived in the area a year later, in February 1832. Downes dispatched a landing party of 282 men, who burned the ships in the harbor and seized the forts on shore. Then he opened a general bombardment of the town until local leaders raised the white flag. The chiefs pledged never again to interfere with American shipping, but occasional piratical attacks continued, and six years later, in January 1837, a second expedition to Quallah Battoo by the frigate *Columbia* and the sloop *John Adams* produced similar results. These punitive expeditions were generally popular in America, when they were noted at all. In the nineteenth century few Americans mourned the deaths of a few hundred natives in a faraway place they had never heard of.

The slave trade

If duty in the Mediterranean was the most pleasant, and service against pirates was the most exciting, duty in the African Squadron was the most despised. This was due mainly to the uncomfortable and even perilous conditions along what was called the Guinea coast, where the weather was oppressive and disease was rampant. Malaria in particular, then believed to be carried by the hot winds blowing off the African coast, was responsible for scores of deaths on U.S. ships. In addition the duty itself— stopping and searching slave ships filled with their human cargo—was repellant, even if it occasionally meant liberation for those on board.

Congress had declared the importation of slaves from Africa illegal after January 1, 1808, though there was no serious effort to interdict that human traffic until 1821, when the navy established an African Squadron. Almost at once, however, its mission became controversial. In part this was because the navy found the work so revolting, but an additional factor was the sectional dispute over the Missouri Compromise (1819–21), which made southern representatives sensitive to implied criticisms of slavery as a labor system. After only two years Congress withdrew its support, and the African Squadron ceased to exist. After that only the Royal Navy made any serious effort to suppress the slave trade. The owners of the illicit slave ships saw an opportunity in these circumstances. Aware of how sensitive the Americans were about interference with their ships, slavers of every nationality—or no nationality at all—began flying the Stars and Stripes in order to deter inspection by the British. When the British saw through this ruse and stopped the ships anyway, the United States objected on principle.

This Anglo-American dispute was resolved in the Webster-Ashburton Treaty of 1842, which, in addition to settling several outstanding border issues between the United States and Canada, also dealt with the situation off Africa. By its terms the British pledged to stop searching vessels flying the American flag, and the Americans pledged to police those vessels themselves by maintaining a naval squadron off Africa that consisted of a force of "not less than eighty guns." In 1843 Oliver Hazard Perry's younger brother, Matthew Calbraith Perry, commanded the first American squadron sent to Africa under this new requirement. While Perry's ships did stop and search a number of illegal slave ships, his orders from the secretary of the navy made it clear that his primary mission was to ensure that the British kept their word and left American merchantmen alone. Moreover, like U.S. Navy squadron commanders elsewhere, Perry also punished local rulers who, in his view, infringed on American rights or attacked American citizens.

Exploring new worlds

In addition to suppressing pirates and protecting American interests around the world, the U.S. Navy of the early nineteenth century also engaged in exploration and scientific investigation. Lieutenant Matthew Fontaine Maury, barred from sea duty by a leg injury, spent most of his career studying ships' logs in order to track the oceans' currents and prevailing wind patterns. His resulting charts brought him international recognition as the Pathfinder of the Seas. The U.S. government also sponsored a number of voyages aimed at advancing geographic and scientific knowledge.

The largest of these was the Great United States Exploring Expedition, which got under way in August 1838 and spent four years circumnavigating the globe. Lieutenant Charles Wilkes commanded the expedition, and though he proved to be an unpopular martinet, it resulted in a number of signal accomplishments. One was confirmation that there was a seventh continent at the South Pole, and a section of Antarctica is still named Wilkes Land. Another was the acquisition of a large number of curious specimens from the South Seas that subsequently made up much of the original collection of the new Smithsonian Institution, established in 1846. Overall the expedition covered eighty-five thousand miles and charted 280 islands, most of them in the South Pacific, as well as mapping about 1,500 miles of the Antarctic coastline.

Commercially the most important of the navy's overseas expeditions in this era was the one led by Matthew Perry to Japan in 1852–54. In command of two steam frigates, the propeller-driven *Mississippi* and the paddle-steamer *Susquehanna*, plus some smaller ships, Perry demonstrated that the navy could serve not only as a tool for chastising natives but also as an effective instrument of American diplomacy. By exercising a combination of firmness and patience, Perry successfully concluded an agreement in which the reclusive Japanese government pledged to protect shipwrecked mariners, to allow foreign ships to re-coal at selected ports, and to open conversations about establishing commercial relations. The ensuing Treaty of Kanagawa (1854) proved to be the opening wedge that brought Japan into the modern world.

Evolving navy culture

Several events in this era contributed to a modest sea change in the character of the officer and enlisted force. Until the 1840s a young man became an officer in the U.S. Navy by being appointed a midshipman as a teenager and learning on the job while at sea. When he felt ready, he took an exam, which, if passed, made him a passed midshipman eligible for appointment to lieutenant when a vacancy occurred. With the emergence of steam engines as well as larger and more complex ordnance, aspiring officers had to master more technical and theoretical subjects. It was partly because of this that the U.S. Naval Academy was established at Annapolis, Maryland, in 1845, forty-three years after the U.S. Military Academy at West Point opened its doors, though the Naval Academy did not initiate a four-year program until 1853.

The enlisted force too was changing. From the very beginning the only qualification for service as a sailor in the U.S. Navy was a strong back. Most of the work on board ships in the Age of Sail consisted of moving heavy objects either by block and tackle or by brute force, and anyone who could pull on a rope or wrestle with a gun—and who could tolerate the severe discipline—was welcome. This often made for a polyglot crew, and U.S. Navy ships generally had large contingents of foreigners, Native Americans, and free blacks, as well as American citizens. The numbers are hard to pin down with precision, but during the Age of Sail perhaps 15 percent of the navy's enlisted force was African American. During the sectional feuding of the 1830s and 1840s, pressure from southern congressmen reduced the number of blacks in the navy to around 10 percent, but it rose again during the Civil War to as high as 20 percent.

Another change during the 1850s was the abolition of flogging, the beating of a bound sailor by a petty officer who wielded a short whip with nine knotted ropes called a cat-of-nine-tails. Given the rough character of the enlisted force, physical punishment was the standard penalty for a wide variety of major and minor infractions, and ship captains could prescribe anywhere from a dozen to a hundred lashes depending on the seriousness of the offense. For most such punishments all hands were called to bear witness in the belief that this offered a profound deterrent to future misconduct. It was unquestionably barbarous, but also effective, and it had been a part of naval life for more than a century. Nevertheless in September 1850 Congress declared it illegal. Though many senior officers grumbled about the ban, it stuck, and punishments afterward consisted of the denial of shore liberty, confinement in irons, or a loss of pay.

A decade later, in the midst of the Civil War, the U.S. Navy abolished another long-standing tradition, this one much beloved by the enlisted sailors. This was the daily grog ration: a half pint of rum or whisky, cut with water, that was issued to every sailor on board, even teenagers, once a day. Though the tradition was common to all navies and predated American independence, the United States was the first nation to abolish it, on September 1, 1862. Spirits continued to be served in the officers' mess until 1914, when Navy Secretary Josephus Daniels put a stop to that too, and the U.S. Navy became "dry."

Manifest destiny and war with Mexico

The years between 1820 and 1850 also marked a surge in American nationalism. The perceived victory in the war with Britain and the so-called Era of Good Feelings that followed fed a national consensus that the United States occupied a special place in history and was destined to be both an example for the world (the City on a Hill) and master of the western hemisphere. This latter notion contributed not only to a general westward migration but also to active efforts to consolidate and expand American sovereignty generally.

In Florida, which the United States obtained from Spain in the Adams-Onis Treaty of 1819, the United States fought a messy and frustrating war with the Seminole Indians between 1835 and 1842. The navy's role in that conflict was mostly to move troops along the coast and up various rivers, though it also conducted expeditions deep into the interior, including one into the heart of the Everglades, where these swamp sailors encountered swarms of mosquitoes and what one described as "a sea of mud." After years of frustrating and costly combat, the war ended in a draw. The government decided simply to ignore those elusive Seminoles who refused removal to the West and declared the war at an end.

While the United States fought the Seminoles in Florida, Texans won their independence from Mexico, and almost at once they began to petition for admission to the Union. Aware that Mexico had never fully accepted Texas independence and concerned that adding Texas to the national domain would reignite the sectional dispute over slavery, Congress demurred. In 1845, however, the expansionist James K. Polk administration pushed through a Texas statehood bill. In the aftermath the Mexican government disputed the location of the Texas-Mexico border, insisting that the Nueces River, and not the Rio Grande, was the actual boundary. When patrols from the two countries collided in the disputed area, Polk called for war.

The Mexican-American War (1846–48) was essentially a land war. Indeed the tiny Mexican Navy consisted of only two seagoing warships, and recognizing that they could have no possible impact on the war, the Mexicans sold them to Britain when the war began. The U.S. Navy thus found itself in the unprecedented position of being a superior naval power in a foreign war. One large naval squadron, initially commanded by Commodore David Connor but subsequently and more effectively under Matthew Perry, operated along the Gulf coast of Mexico, while another, much smaller squadron operated along the California coast.

The largest and most important naval operation of the war was the successful landing of an American army that eventually numbered some ten thousand men on the coast of Mexico near Vera Cruz in the spring of 1847. In the first large-scale amphibious operation in American history, soldiers from army transports climbed down into smaller surfboats and were rowed to the beach by navy sailors. Vera Cruz surrendered after a two-week siege, and Major General Winfield Scott began a decisive campaign to

Mexico City, where U.S. Marines from the fleet stood guard in the "halls of Montezuma."

The success of American arms in the war with Mexico added more than half a million square miles to the national domain, including all of what is now California, Nevada, Arizona, and New Mexico, plus parts of Utah and Colorado. It did little, however, to affect American military or naval policy. Though professional officers had commanded the American armies, volunteer soldiers did most of the fighting, which confirmed the American commitment to a militia army. Similarly, though the U.S. Navy had performed satisfactorily, there had been no celebrated naval triumphs, and the navy remained both small by European standards and marginal to American policymakers.

Chapter 5
Steam and iron: the Civil War navy (1850–1865)

Even while the war with Mexico was in progress, a national debate over whether slavery should be allowed into the land acquired as a result of that war ignited sectional animosity that threatened to tear the country apart. A compromise hammered out in 1850 pleased few, and for the next decade the issue of slavery's future affected nearly every aspect of American politics and government. That same decade witnessed a virtual technological revolution that affected large segments of American society and also transformed the tools of war. Thus the Civil War that began in the spring of 1861 saw the introduction of the military use of the telegraph and the railroad and the adoption of the rifled musket, with grooves cut into the inside of the barrel to put a spin on the projectile and thereby dramatically increase both range and accuracy. At sea the new technology included steam propulsion, iron armor, and exploding shells fired from ever-larger naval guns, many of them rifled. The Civil War also saw the first widespread use of what were then called torpedoes and later known as mines.

A technological transformation

For more than two centuries naval warships had changed little. Wooden-hull ships propelled by sails carried muzzle-loaded iron gun tubes that fired solid shot. By 1850, however, that was changing, and changing swiftly. Matthew Perry had commanded steam ships during the operations off Vera Cruz in 1847 and during his expedition to Japan in 1852. Over the ensuing decade steam ships became more ubiquitous as they became more efficient. Naval guns became much larger, measured less often by the weight of their cannon balls (e.g., 24-pounders) than by the size of their muzzles (e.g., six inches). Like the army's shoulder arms, many of the navy's new gun barrels were rifled, and the projectiles they fired were no longer merely solid iron balls but explosive shells. All of this occurred just in time to have a dramatic influence on the navies that fought in the American Civil War.

Though a steam vessel had begun passenger service on the Hudson River as early as 1807, the United States lagged behind European powers in adopting this new technology for its warships. One restraint was that early steam engines were remarkably inefficient, often generating only a few miles of forward progress for each ton of coal burned. In addition, however, U.S. Navy squadrons often operated three to five thousand miles from an American port where they could re-coal, making them utterly dependent on others for fuel. This logistical constraint did not affect British ships in the same way because Britain had bases all around the world.

The United States did produce the world's first propeller-driven warship, the USS *Princeton*, designed by the Swedish immigrant John Ericsson. It was launched in 1843, a few months ahead of the British *Rattlesnake*, which also boasted a screw propeller. American enthusiasm for innovation was muted, however, when the explosion of one of the *Princeton*'s experimental large-caliber guns during a public relations cruise in 1844 killed the secretary of state and secretary of the navy.

Nevertheless by the 1850s lawmakers recognized that the nation's wooden sailing navy, much of it left over from the War of 1812, was growing increasingly obsolete, and as a result Congress passed a number of bills to modernize the navy. The turning point came in 1854. The year before, Congress authorized funds to build the nation's last all-sail warship, the USS *Constellation*, named in honor of one of the original Humphreys frigates. The very next year, however, Congress turned a technological page and authorized six new steam-powered frigates. Indeed in the five years between 1854 and 1859, that is, between the Kansas-Nebraska Act and John Brown's raid on Harpers Ferry, the U.S. Navy was dramatically transformed by the addition of twenty-four major new combatants, all of them steamers and all armed with the latest and most sophisticated naval ordnance. It was the largest peacetime naval expansion since the Naval Act of 1816. Thus, though the U.S. Navy remained small by European standards, when the Civil War began, more than half of the forty-two ships on active service were of the newest and most efficient type.

By contrast, the Confederate States began the Civil War with no navy at all, and the South embraced the traditional policies of the weaker naval power: harbor defense and commerce raiding. The Confederates also sought to discover and employ technological innovations that would enable them to offset the North's overwhelming superiority in conventional naval power.

The Anaconda Plan and the naval blockade

By far the most ambitious undertaking of the U.S. Navy during the Civil War was its blockade of the Confederate coast. In May 1861 General Winfield Scott outlined a plan for the suppression of the rebellion that included a naval blockade, a holding action in northern Virginia, and a campaign along the axis of the Mississippi River. Northern critics who were eager to crush the rebellion at once found this program too passive and dubbed it the Anaconda Plan, a derisive reference to a South American reptile that slowly strangled its prey. Even before Scott articulated that vision, however, President Abraham Lincoln had announced a blockade of the Confederate coast, doing so on April 19, 1861, only five days after the first shots of the war were fired at Fort Sumter in Charleston Harbor.

Both at the time and subsequently, many questioned Lincoln's use of the term *blockade*, which seemed to imply that the Confederate states constituted a foreign belligerent rather than a rebellious section of the United States, as Lincoln consistently maintained. Moreover the declaration appeared monumentally ambitious, even preposterous. International law held that no blockade was legally binding unless there was a naval squadron physically present off the coast to enforce it, and it was hard to imagine how a navy of only forty-two ships could blockade a coastline that was 3,500 miles long. As a result Lincoln's proclamation provoked skepticism in Europe and ridicule in the South.

To make the blockade a reality, the United States embarked on an unprecedented naval expansion. Between 1861 and 1865 the Union navy increased from forty-two ships to more than six hundred. Most of the new ships were converted merchant steamers since it was much quicker and cheaper to modify an existing vessel to wartime use than to build a new ship from the keel up. Often this transformation involved little more than strengthening the decks to bear the weight of the naval guns and adding a magazine below the water line. These converted vessels were unlikely to contend successfully with the warships of European navies, but they were more than sufficient to catch or deter unarmed blockade-runners.

Manning this greatly enlarged navy was another challenge. Officers who had languished for two decades or more at the rank of lieutenant found themselves elevated swiftly to command positions, and new volunteer officers became instant lieutenants. The enlisted force grew from a few thousand to over a hundred thousand. Some were farm boys seeking adventure; some hoped to avoid service in the expanding army, especially after conscription was enacted in 1863. Many had never seen the ocean. Free blacks had always constituted a part of the navy's enlisted force, and now former slaves, called "contrabands" in the parlance of the day, enlisted as well. Many of these were escaped slaves who flagged down U.S. Navy vessels off the South Atlantic coast and asked to join the crew. Starved for manpower as they were, most officers simply added their names to the ship's roster.

In June 1861 a Navy Department circular established the designator "nurse." Though these positions were intended to be filled entirely by men, a handful of women also served as nurses, both on hospital ships and in navy hospitals ashore. Aside from that, the U.S. Navy remained an all-male service through the nineteenth century.

By the end of 1861 the Union had more than two hundred ships on the blockade, and while southern blockade-runners still got through with annoying regularity, the tightening grip on the southern coastline soon began to affect the South's economy. While the Confederacy managed to import an impressive amount of munitions to sustain its field armies, the blockade fueled inflation, depressed civilian morale, and contributed to a growing war weariness among the southern population.

The clash of ironclads

Aware that the South could never match the North in terms of the number of ships it produced, the Confederate secretary of the navy, Stephen R. Mallory, sought a technological shortcut: an iron-armored ship that by itself could neutralize a whole fleet of wooden warships. The steam frigate *Merrimack* had been abandoned by the U.S. Navy when it evacuated Norfolk, and atop its hull Confederate authorities constructed a squat superstructure with sloping wooden walls that were two feet thick covered by two layers of two-inch iron plate. The designers also attached a 1,500-pound ram to its prow. The reconfigured vessel, armed with ten heavy guns, was rechristened the CSS *Virginia.*

In Washington, Union Navy Secretary Gideon Welles was aware of the conversion of the *Merrimack* into the *Virginia.* In response he appointed an Ironclad Board to consider proposals for a Union counterweapon, and one of the three designs subsequently accepted by this board was that of John Ericsson. His design called for a vessel with a flat deck barely above the waterline, in the center of which was a cylindrical rotating tower containing two enormous 11-inch guns. With some skepticism the Ironclad Board awarded Ericsson a contract that required him to complete this vessel, eventually dubbed the *Monitor*, in only one hundred days. Ericsson beat that deadline by seven days, though last-minute adjustments and testing took another few weeks; as a result the *Monitor* did not leave New York for Hampton Roads, Virginia, until March 6, 1862. As it happened, she would be late by exactly one day.

On March 8, while the *Monitor* was en route from New York, the *Virginia*, under the command of Captain Franklin Buchanan, emerged from her dry dock in the Portsmouth Navy Yard and steamed out into Hampton Roads. Buchanan directed his balky vessel across the roadstead toward the wooden-hull sailing frigate USS *Cumberland* and smashed the *Virginia*'s iron ram deep into her starboard side. Down in the *Virginia*'s fire room, the ship's engineer, E. A. Jack, felt "a tremor throughout the ship, and [he] was nearly thrown from the coal bucket upon which [he] was sitting." The *Cumberland* began to sink almost at once, going down with her guns firing and her flag flying. Buchanan then directed the fire of his ship's ten guns at the nearby USS *Congress*, which caught fire and later exploded in a giant fireball. In a single day one Confederate ironclad had sunk two U.S. Navy warships and killed 240 American sailors, the worst one-day loss in U.S. Navy history until World War II.

That night, near midnight, the USS *Monitor* arrived in Hampton Roads, and the next morning the two ironclads engaged one another for four hours, during which they often fought hull-to-hull. Neither ship was able to inflict serious damage on the other, and the outcome was a tactical draw. Nevertheless the arrival of the *Monitor* had effectively neutralized the offensive potential of the *Virginia* and allowed the Union navy to retain its position in

Hampton Roads. A few weeks later, when U.S. Army forces compelled the Confederates to evacuate Norfolk, the southern ironclad lost her base, and Confederate authorities destroyed her to prevent her from falling into the hands of the Yankees.

Over the next three years both sides built more ironclad warships. In that arms race the Union had all the advantages, for it had a far more robust maritime infrastructure. The Confederacy laid down a total of fifty ironclads though many of them never got to sea for lack of engines, or armor, or both. One Confederate innovation was the submarine *H. L. Hunley*. Built initially with private funds, it was taken over by the Confederate government and manned by volunteers. On February 17, 1864, the *Hunley* crept out of Charleston Harbor and sank the blockading ship USS *Housatonic*, though the submarine's entire crew was also lost. Such innovations notwithstanding, the Union could, and did, simply outbuild the Confederacy. Before the war was over, the Union produced more than sixty monitor-type ironclads, each class of them larger and more powerfully armed than the one before.

The advent of iron-armored warships during the Civil War fell short of being a full-scale technological revolution. Ever thicker armor led to ever larger naval guns, until it became evident that to make a ship invulnerable would render her virtually immobile. Armor continued to be used in warship construction after the war, but it was applied selectively, to protect engine spaces or magazines. The *Monitor*'s rotating turret proved a more durable innovation and characterized warship construction well into the twenty-first century.

Confederate commerce raiding

Commerce raiding was the traditional recourse for nations engaged in wars with superior naval powers. Though privateering had been the most effective form of commerce raiding in America's earlier wars, that option was not available to the

Confederates because the Union blockade made it all but impossible for privateersmen to bring their prizes into southern ports to be condemned, and a British declaration of neutrality closed British ports to them as well. That removed the profit motive, so would-be privateersmen turned instead to blockade running. As a result Confederate commerce raiding had to be conducted by warships of the small Confederate navy, most of which were obtained surreptitiously from British builders.

The most prominent of these raiders was the CSS *Alabama*. Commanded by Captain (later Rear Admiral) Raphael Semmes, the *Alabama* conducted a two-year cruise over three oceans, during which it captured sixty-eight prizes. Since Semmes could not send those prizes into port, he burned them, using four of them to rid himself of his accumulated prisoners. The *Alabama* also fought and sank the USS *Hatteras* in the Gulf of Mexico in January 1863, which was the first time a steam-powered warship sank another steam warship in battle. The *Alabama* was finally cornered in Cherbourg, France, in June 1864 by the USS *Kearsarge*, commanded by Captain John A. Winslow. After an hour-long battle the *Alabama* sank just outside French territorial waters, though Semmes himself and most of his officers escaped to a nearby British yacht.

Another famous Confederate raider was the CSS *Shenandoah*, commanded by James I. Waddell, which Mallory sent to the north Pacific to attack the American whaling fleet there. After a six-month cruise around the Cape of Good Hope, across the Indian Ocean, and into the Pacific, Waddell caught and destroyed twenty-three American whaling ships in the Bering Sea in the spring and summer of 1865. Not until August 9 did Waddell learn that the war had ended in April. Fearing that he might be hanged as a pirate, he decided to take his ship back to Liverpool, England, where he arrived in November 1865, thirteen months after he had set out and seven months after the Confederate surrender at Appomattox.

While it did not affect the outcome of the war, Confederate commerce raiding did inflict a disproportionate amount of damage on Union shipping for a relatively small investment. Altogether Confederate commerce raiders captured and destroyed some 284 U.S. merchant ships. After the war the United States protested to the British that their complicity in building and fitting out the raiders had prolonged the war. Britain agreed to arbitration, and in 1871 an Anglo-American tribunal awarded the United States $15.5 million for the destruction wrought by the commerce raiders.

The river war

The U.S. Navy also played an important, even indispensable role in the campaign on the western rivers—the Cumberland, the Tennessee, and especially the Mississippi. An essential element of any riverine campaign is close cooperation between the army and navy commanders, but during the Civil War there was no established protocol for such cooperation, which meant that success depended heavily on the willingness of the two services to work together. For the most part this proved adequate.

As in the saltwater war, the Union had the necessary resources to construct specially designed armored warships for the western rivers. Bridge builder James Buchanan Eads designed ironclads with flat bottoms that, despite their great weight, could maneuver in relatively shallow water. These vessels played an important role in the Union seizure of Fort Henry on the Tennessee River in February 1862, and the capture of Island Number Ten on the Mississippi River in April. In the Battle of Memphis in June, the wooden vessels of the Confederate River Defense Fleet were all but annihilated.

Meanwhile, at the southern end of the Mississippi, Flag Officer David Glasgow Farragut led his oceangoing wooden warships past the large masonry forts guarding the approach to New Orleans, fought a spirited engagement with the Confederate defense fleet, and compelled the surrender of the South's largest city on April 25, 1862. Farragut became America's first rear admiral and was subsequently elevated to the rank of full admiral. By the spring of 1862, Union naval forces had seized control of both ends of the Mississippi River. Only the Confederate citadel of Vicksburg, Mississippi, held the two halves of the Confederacy together.

The Union campaign to seize Vicksburg lasted most of a year and was marked by a number of false starts and disappointments. Then, in the spring of 1863, Farragut's foster brother, Rear Admiral David Dixon Porter, led a portion of his river fleet past the Vicksburg batteries in order to transport the soldiers of Grant's army across the river so they could approach Vicksburg from the east. That proved decisive, and after a dramatic campaign ashore and a lengthy siege of the city, Vicksburg surrendered on July 4, 1863. After that, as Lincoln put it, the Father of Waters once more flowed "unvexed to the sea."

The battle against the shore

Part of the Union blockading strategy was the seizure of ports along the Confederate coastline. This began early, with the capture of Port Royal, South Carolina, in November 1861, and continued throughout the war. By 1864 only three major port cities remained in Confederate hands: Mobile, Alabama; Charleston, South Carolina; and Wilmington, North Carolina. These proved especially resilient not only because of local geography but also because of the threat of Confederate mines, or what were then called torpedoes. The widespread employment of underwater mines was one of several portents that the Civil War marked a change not only in technology but also in military ethics. Placing explosive devices in the path of the enemy, like wrecking railroads or destroying private property, had been all but unthinkable in 1861, yet by 1864 they had become routine. Along with the threat of ironclads, the use of underwater mines constituted a new danger for the blockaders and a significant shift in the character of naval warfare.

In August 1864 Farragut effectively closed Mobile Bay to blockade-runners when he charged into the bay, damning the torpedoes, and defeated the rebel ironclad *Tennessee*. Charleston proved tougher; it did not fall until late in 1864, when it was cut off by General William Tecumseh Sherman after his March to the Sea. Wilmington, defended by an enormous earthwork called Fort Fisher that guarded the entrance into the Cape Fear River, was the last holdout. Fort Fisher fell in January 1865 following a furious naval bombardment by no less than forty-four Union navy warships and an overland assault by Union army forces assisted by a landing party of sailors and marines. This cut off the last source of external supplies for the Confederate army defending Richmond. Four months later Lee's beleaguered army evacuated the Confederate capital and began its march to Appomattox Court House.

4. In this painting by William Overend, David Glasgow Farragut appears almost nonchalant as he presides over the Battle of Mobile Bay on August 5, 1864. Alongside Farragut's flagship USS *Hartford* is the dark hull of the Confederate ironclad *Tennessee*. This was the battle in which Farragut damned the torpedoes as he charged into Mobile Bay.

The Union navy played a conspicuous and essential role in the final victory, and by the spring of 1865, when Lee surrendered his army to Grant, the navy had grown to sixteen times its prewar size and boasted some of the most advanced warships in the world.

Chapter 6
The doldrums and the new navy (1865–1900)

Sailors refer to those areas near the equator in both the Atlantic and the Pacific where the prevailing winds are calm and unreliable as "the doldrums." In the Age of Sail ships could find themselves becalmed there for days or even weeks. It is therefore an appropriate term to describe the U.S. Navy during the two decades after the end of the Civil War: an era of swift retrenchment with little forward progress. When the Civil War ended, the U.S. Navy boasted a total of 671 warships, all but a few of them steamers, many of them ironclads, and some that were the most advanced of their type. Yet within a decade all but a few dozen had been sold off, scrapped, or placed in ordinary—mothballed for a future crisis. Conforming to the now familiar pattern, after a dramatic expansion to meet a crisis, the navy swiftly contracted at almost the moment the crisis ended. By 1870 the U.S. Navy had only fifty-two ships on active service.

Champions of a large standing navy generally condemned this contraction. It seemed to them that the United States had been on the brink of establishing itself as a world naval power only to let the moment slip away as the country relapsed into semi-isolationism. However, among the 671 navy warships that existed in 1865 were 418 converted merchantmen and more than a hundred river ironclads—ships that were unlikely to affect the global balance of naval power in the postwar era. Fifty-two of the

671 were monitors with their characteristic rotating turret, yet given their low silhouette and marginal buoyancy, they were unsuited to service in the open ocean. Like Jefferson's gunboats, they were useful primarily for coastal defense, and like the gunboats, most of them were laid up in ordinary to await a future crisis.

Retrenchment

Part of the reason for the swift cutbacks was simple economy. The Civil War had been hugely expensive, and the nation had gone heavily into debt to pay for it. In addition Americans continued to look mostly inward in the postwar era, toward the South, where Reconstruction dominated national politics, and to the West, where the Homestead Act of 1862 made free land available and where the completion of the transcontinental railroad in 1869 made those lands more accessible than ever.

In addition to reducing the number of ships, the navy also appeared to be willing to abandon at least some of the new wartime technology. While steam power and iron armor had characterized much of the Navy's wartime fleet, after 1865 the warships that resumed the duty of patrolling distant stations overseas were wooden-hulled and unarmored. Though they all possessed steam engines as well as masts and sails, they navigated most of the time under sail power alone because the United States still lacked secure overseas bases where its warships could refuel. The country acquired its first overseas possession in 1867, when it annexed the unpopulated atoll of Midway in the Pacific, but aside from that it had to rely on bases controlled by foreign powers. Unwilling to become dependent on others for fuel, American warships relied primarily on wind power and used their steam engines only in emergencies. As a result they were known as "auxiliary steamers," and captains were sometimes required to defend in writing a decision to light the boilers.

These auxiliary steamers reprised their prewar roles of protecting American merchant shipping overseas and representing the nation abroad. Though a number of submarine telegraphic cables now made possible swifter communication between Washington and other world capitals, the lack of wireless telegraphy meant that U.S. Navy captains at sea remained all but sovereign when serving on these distant stations. As they had before the war, they authorized or led occasional expeditions ashore to punish bad behavior or to subdue perceived threats. Though such expeditions were never directed toward a European power, it was universally understood that Western navies could punish non-Europeans without consequence. In the five years after Appomattox, U.S. Navy officers sent landing parties ashore in Formosa, Japan, Uruguay, Mexico, Panama, and Korea. The Korean landing in May and June 1871 was one of the largest. Rear Admiral John Rodgers (son of the John Rodgers of the War of 1812) had been dispatched to Korea in the hope of opening the "Hermit Kingdom" to Western trade, as Matthew Perry had done with Japan twenty years earlier. When Korean forts fired on his ships, Rodgers demanded an apology, and when it was not forthcoming, he landed a party of 684 men who stormed the fort and killed 243 Koreans. Rodgers behaved fully in the nineteenth-century tradition, but he also failed in his mission. Not until 1878, when Commodore Robert W. Shufeldt arrived in the USS *Ticonderoga,* did the United States begin to lay the groundwork for an eventual trade agreement with Korea that was ratified in 1883.

Occasionally it was evident that the lack of a robust naval force could limit the nation's ability to influence events abroad. In 1873 the Spanish Navy captured the side-wheel steamer *Virginius,* which was engaged in running arms and supplies to rebel groups in Cuba, and took it into Santiago Harbor, where the officers and crew were tried as pirates and sentenced to die by firing squad. Though the ship was Cuban owned, it flew an American flag, and her captain was a U.S. citizen named Joseph Fry. Most of those on board were American or British citizens who either sympathized with the Cuban rebels or who were in it for the money—or both. Fifty of them, including Fry, were shot before Sir Lambdon Lorraine, commanding HMS *Niobe*, threatened to bombard Santiago unless the executions were halted.

News of the executions provoked widespread outrage in the United States, and the Ulysses S. Grant administration demanded an explanation from Spain. At the same time, Grant also ordered the navy to prepare for war, more to underscore his seriousness than to engage in actual hostilities. The incident was eventually resolved peacefully when the Spanish agreed to pay an indemnity to the families of the slain, yet the haphazard mobilization effort revealed the appalling unreadiness of the U.S. Navy to fight a European power, even a declining European power such as Spain.

Straws in the wind

The revival of the U.S. Navy in the last two decades of the nineteenth century resulted from a variety of circumstances. The most immediate was the simple fact that the several dozen ships retained from the Civil War were getting so old that they had become antiques. Indeed the British wit Oscar Wilde made the U.S. Navy the butt of a joke in an 1887 story entitled "The Canterville Ghost." When an American character in Wilde's story asserts that the United States has no ruins or curiosities like those found in Europe, the ghost of the story's title replies, "No ruins! No curiosities! You have your Navy and your manners."

If the U.S. Navy was not quite a "ruin" in the 1880s, it was evident that thirty-year-old warships could no longer carry out the nation's overseas duties efficiently. In 1883 therefore Congress authorized the construction of three new cruisers and one dispatch vessel, its first important naval appropriation since Appomattox. Because these ships were subsequently christened *Atlanta*, *Boston*, *Chicago*, and *Dolphin*, they came to be known as the ABCD ships. Though they still carried masts and spars for sailing, they also incorporated most of the new technologies that European navies had embraced over the previous twenty years, including steel hulls with watertight compartments and an electrical system to replace the use of lanterns below decks. Their construction did not, however, mark a significant change in national naval policy, for the missions assigned to these new ships were the same as those of the "auxiliary steamers" they replaced.

Nevertheless other straws in the wind suggested that a true revolution was coming. In October 1884, Commodore Stephen B. Luce founded the U.S. Naval War College in Newport, Rhode Island. There, middle-grade navy officers studied not only the new technology but also the more philosophical subject of naval strategy. Opponents of a standing peacetime navy had long argued that a permanent naval establishment would generate a class of self-perpetuating senior officers—a naval aristocracy—that would constitute, by its very existence, a threat to democratic values. The founding of the Naval War College was significant therefore not merely because of its official role of preparing senior officers for command positions but also because it demonstrated that this long-standing prejudice was weakening.

At the same time, the enlisted force of the U.S. Navy became less eclectic and international. The smaller size of the navy meant that recruiters could be more selective, and the steam engine plants and long-range guns required greater technical knowledge than had been needed during the Age of Sail. This resulted in a concerted effort to recruit U.S. citizens and train them ashore in specialized schools before sending them to the fleet to learn on the job, as had been common practice in all navies for centuries.

Another harbinger of change came in 1886, when Congress approved the construction of the first U.S. warships to bear the designation "battleship." The two ships were subsequently named *Maine* and *Texas*, beginning a tradition of naming battleships for states. Like the ABCD ships, however, this was another false dawn, for not only were the ships relatively small for battleships (at 6,300 and 6,600 tons, respectively); they were also "short-legged," that is, designed primarily for coastal operations. The assumption that a naval force could be quickly conjured up in an emergency remained a central argument in the annual report of Secretary of the Navy Benjamin Franklin Tracy in 1889. Tracy conceded that the navy was hardly thriving. "The wooden ships are a makeshift," he wrote. "The old monitors are worse than useless." He concluded, "At no previous time in the present century has the country been relatively so powerless at sea." Yet Tracy clung to the traditional view that the U.S. Navy should be "adapted to defensive war," and (quoting John Adams) that it should be a navy that could be "quickly brought into use." It was a view that had dominated U.S. naval policy for more than a century, but it was about to change.

The new navy

If there was a single moment in history when the United States abandoned its historic commitment to a militia navy and embraced the idea of a standing peacetime navy, that moment was in 1890, when the confluence of three developments produced a sea change. The first of these was a congressional decision to fund three new battleships, subsequently named *Indiana*, *Massachusetts*, and *Oregon*. Displacing ten thousand tons each, they were much larger than the *Maine* or the *Texas* authorized just four years earlier, and they had a more modern look as well, with massive 13-inch rifled guns housed in giant turrets fore and aft. More significant, they were not replacement vessels for aging auxiliary steamers but true seagoing battleships whose primary mission was to fight and defeat other battleships. They were numbered BB-1, BB-2, and BB-3, implying that there could well be others to follow.

The second event of 1890 was the publication of a book burdened with the rather cumbersome title of *The Influence of Sea Power upon History, 1660–1783*. The work of a previously little known navy captain named Alfred Thayer Mahan, who had spent the previous three years lecturing at the new Naval War College, the book was an analysis of how the relatively small nation of Great Britain had managed to evolve into the most powerful country in Europe and arguably the most powerful in the world, with a global empire on which, as the saying went, the sun never set. The British had been able to do all this, Mahan explained, by seizing command of the seas with its battleship fleet (ships of the line). From that single circumstance flowed all the rest: the wealth that came from trade, the power that came with wealth, and military dominance. Moreover Mahan presented this remarkable achievement as a kind of blueprint, appending a general introduction to the book that itemized the preconditions of naval dominance, and implying (at least) that nations possessing these characteristics could duplicate Britain's rise to power.

The third circumstance that fed the naval revolution of 1890 was the U.S. census report of that year, which noted the disappearance of the western frontier, suggesting that America's future growth might extend beyond the boundaries of her continental limits. The construction of the new battleships and the widespread popularity of Mahan's book seemed to offer both the means and the rationale for the United States to accept the challenge and to duplicate Britain's success. Mahan's book did not cause a change in U.S. naval policy, but it provided an intellectual rationale and justification for a policy that was already evolving.

By 1896 all five of America's new battleships had been completed and launched, and a sixth (the *Iowa*) joined them a year later. None of these ships had been built to meet a perceived crisis or a national emergency. Instead the United States had finally embraced the navalist argument that a mature nation-state required a naval force of the first rank. Soon enough circumstances would offer an opportunity to test both the ships and the theory.

A splendid little war

For more than a quarter of a century Americans had watched events in Spanish Cuba with varying degrees of concern and disapproval. In 1873 the United States had declined to go to war with Spain over the interception of the *Virginius*, but unrest in the island continued, and a new outbreak of violence in 1895 led the Spanish to adopt more draconian countermeasures against the rebellious elements. American newspapers deplored the new tactics, and in 1898 President William McKinley approved the suggestion of America's consul general in Cuba to send one of America's new battleships to Havana on a courtesy visit as a signal of American concern. The ship McKinley sent was the USS *Maine*.

On the night of February 15, 1898, the *Maine* was quietly at anchor in Havana Harbor when an explosion sent her to the bottom, taking 260 Americans down with her. Though the cause of this disaster was eventually determined to be the detonation of coal dust in the bunkers, Americans at the time believed that the Spanish had somehow destroyed the ship. That assumption led to a popular clamor for war, a clamor that McKinley was unable to resist, and the United States declared war against Spain on April 25, 1898.

The United States had not fought a European opponent since the War of 1812. Though impressive by national standards, its new navy paled next to those of Britain, France, or even Germany. Spain's navy, however, once the greatest in the world, was now a mere shadow of its former self. Nor was Spain's heart in the struggle. In effect the upward trajectory of American naval expansion had crossed the downward trajectory of Spanish retreat from great power status.

From the U.S. Navy's point of view, the war with Spain in 1898 was, in the words of Secretary of State John Hay, "a splendid little war." Active hostilities lasted barely six months and were punctuated by two entirely one-sided naval engagements on opposite sides of the world that seemed to validate both the decision to build the new battleships and Mahan's theory about the wellspring of national greatness.

The first of those battles took place on May 1, 1898, in Manila Bay in the Philippines, almost exactly halfway around the world from Cuba. One of Mahan's postulates was that it was essential to seize control of the sea at the outset of any war by destroying the enemy's principal battle fleets. Since Spain had a small naval squadron in the Philippines, Commodore George Dewey, commanding the American Asian Squadron at Hong Kong, was ordered to find and destroy it.

He did so in one of the most complete and one-sided naval victories in history. Dewey did not have any of the new U.S. battleships in his squadron, but he had several heavy cruisers, and

5. An artist's depiction of the Battle of Manila Bay, on May 1, 1898, in which Commodore George Dewey's Asiatic Squadron destroyed the Spanish fleet in a single afternoon. It was a turning point for both the U.S. Navy and for the nation, since it led to American occupation of the Philippines and established American interests in the western Pacific.

with them he entered Manila Bay and took the anchored Spanish squadron under fire. In the steamy tropical climate the gunners on the American ships stripped to their waists and bound up their heads in water-soaked rags. They kept their shoes on, however, so that their feet did not burn on the hot deck plates. Down in the fire room, where the temperature neared 200 degrees, the stokers sang, "There'll Be a Hot Time in the Old Town Tonight."

Despite the high morale, American marksmanship was abysmal (only 141 of 5,859 shells actually hit their targets), but Spanish marksmanship was worse, and within a few hours all of the Spanish ships were smoking wrecks. Those few hours successfully eliminated Spanish sea power from the Pacific and led, unavoidably, to the question of what was to be done with Manila and, for that matter, the entire archipelago of the Philippines. In the end McKinley decided that it was the duty of the United States to assume the responsibility and annex the islands.

Two months later, on July 3, the American victory at Manila was matched by a triumph off the south coast of Cuba. Spain had dispatched its Home Squadron from Cádiz to the Caribbean to defend Cuba, but it was soon trapped inside Santiago Harbor by a larger American squadron under Rear Admiral William T. Sampson. The approach of an American land force convinced the Spanish squadron commander, Admiral Pascual Cervera, to make a run for it. As he charged out of the harbor, the American fleet was waiting for him. In a running fight U.S. Navy ships destroyed the entire Spanish squadron, killing three hundred men, wounding five hundred more, and taking 1,800 prisoners. American casualties consisted of one man killed and one wounded.

With the peace treaty signed in Paris in December 1898, Spain granted Cuba its independence, though the United States assumed significant authority on the island and in 1903 negotiated a lease that gave the U.S. Navy control of Guantánamo Bay on Cuba's south coast. Spain also ceded the Philippines,

Puerto Rico, Guam, and Wake Island to the United States, which paid Spain $20 million for them. Separately but simultaneously the annexation of the Kingdom of Hawaii, along with the previous annexation of Midway, gave the United States a series of Pacific Ocean stepping stones, each a potential refueling stop, that led from Hawaii to Midway, to Wake, to Guam, and to the Philippines. It made the United States not merely a continental power but a global power.

Chapter 7

A navy second to none: the U.S. Navy and World War I (1900–1939)

On September 6, 1901, a deranged anarchist shot President McKinley. The president lingered for eight days before dying on September 14. That made Theodore Roosevelt, at age forty-two, the youngest president in American history. "Teddy," as he was often called, had been an enthusiastic navalist since childhood. His thesis at Harvard, a detailed study of the naval engagements of the War of 1812, was subsequently turned into a popular book that remains in print to this day. In 1890 he read and glowingly reviewed Mahan's book, and he served as assistant secretary of the navy during McKinley's first term, before being selected as his running mate in 1900. It is not surprising, therefore, that the U.S. Navy thrived during his administration. Two of the events most closely associated with his presidency are the cruise of the Great White Fleet (1907–9) and the construction of the Panama Canal, which opened for business in 1914, just as Europe was tumbling into war.

The Great White Fleet

Mahan had postulated that battleships, especially battleships operating in a concentrated fleet, were the sine qua non of naval power. In 1902, the first year of Roosevelt's presidency, the United States commissioned one new battleship, which was christened the *Maine* in honor of the one lost in Havana Harbor four years before. A year later the USS *Missouri* was commissioned. Then, between 1906 and 1908, no fewer than thirteen new battleships joined the fleet. After that there was no longer any doubt that the United States had decided to pursue the Mahanian prescription. Even as those new battleships put to sea, however, dramatic changes in ship design were redefining the index of naval power.

The biggest change concerned battleship armament. The USS *New Hampshire*, laid down in May 1905, boasted a main battery of four 12-inch guns plus a secondary battery of smaller guns. For some time ship designers and naval officers had observed that during the early stages of a naval engagement, when the ships were farthest apart, only the largest of their guns would be within range, which made a secondary battery largely irrelevant. When the USS *South Carolina* and USS *Michigan* were laid down in 1906, they each carried a much larger primary battery of eight 12-inch guns, twice as many as the *New Hampshire*. The *South Carolina* and *Michigan* were not completed, however, until 1910, and in the meantime Britain stole a nautical march on the United States—and on everyone else—by hurriedly completing HMS *Dreadnought* in 1906. With ten 12-inch guns and only a small secondary battery, she could bring twice as many guns to bear in the early stages of a battle than any other ship then afloat. From 1906 onward all battleships, of every nation, were classified either as dreadnoughts or pre-dreadnoughts.

Another big change in battleship design during this era was the switch from coal to oil as fuel. Oil generated more power and made ships faster—a critical advantage in battle. For the oil-rich United States this required simply reengineering the power plant. For the British, however, it was a much more serious transition, for while Britain had lots of coal, it possessed almost no domestic oil, which made Britain newly dependent on overseas oil. Britain "solved" this problem by creating the Anglo-Persian Oil Company, though it was a decision that carried the seeds of future complications in the Middle East. The result of these developments was that the modified yardstick of naval power was now the number of oil-burning dreadnoughts a nation possessed.

Elected in his own right in 1904, Roosevelt was eager to test the capabilities of the new, though already superseded, U.S. battleships. To do that he decided to dispatch sixteen of them on a round-the-world cruise. Because all the ships were painted peacetime white, their ensuing circumnavigation has ever since been known as the cruise of the "Great White Fleet." Officially, at least, the purpose of the cruise was to test the ships' capability on long voyages, though Roosevelt also expected significant political and diplomatic benefits. The fifteen-month cruise was a complete success. Logistically the navy learned important lessons about refueling at sea, and the press coverage ashore generated more popular support for the navy. Overseas other naval powers, especially Japan, took due notice of the arrival of the United States on the world stage.

The Panama Canal

Another of Mahan's assertions was that a nation's battle fleet should be kept intact as a single "fleet in being." This was difficult for the United States, which had two coasts separated by a fourteen-thousand-mile journey around Cape Horn. The obvious solution was to build a canal across the Central American isthmus, a dream of mariners since the days of the early explorers. A French company had begun constructing a canal across Panama (then part of Colombia) in the 1880s but had gone bankrupt. In 1903 the United States signed the Hay-Herrán Treaty with Colombia to take over the project. When the Colombian Senate rejected the treaty and demanded more money, investors in the original project helped to engineer a separatist revolution in Panama and appealed to the United States for support. Colombian authorities sought to suppress the rebellion, but the USS *Nashville* interceded to prevent the landing of Colombian troops, and soon thereafter the United States recognized Panama's independence. Almost immediately the Roosevelt administration signed a treaty with the breakaway government that gave the United States control of a ten-mile-wide strip across the isthmus.

Work on the canal began almost at once. It was an enormous undertaking, and Roosevelt himself took particular interest in it, becoming the first president to leave the country while in office when he made a trip to the Canal Zone to inspect progress. The canal opened for business in August 1914, two weeks after the opening shots of the First World War.

The next year saw an important change in the navy bureaucracy. The Board of Navy Commissioners, established in 1815, had been replaced by a decentralized bureau system in 1842. It performed indifferently until the Spanish-American War, after which the navy created something called the General Board to improve centralized planning. The General Board, however, was purely advisory, and it did not provide the kind of command leadership desired by the more progressive naval officers. Rear Admiral Bradley Fiske in particular pressed for the creation of a system modeled on that of the Prussian General Staff. His proposal might have died aborning but for the outbreak of war in Europe, which provided the spur necessary to prod Congress into passing a bill creating the Office of Chief of Naval Operations, and in May 1915 William S. Benson became the first to hold that post.

The U.S. Navy and World War I

The launching of the *Dreadnought* in 1906 helped trigger a naval arms race between Britain and Imperial Germany, one of several factors that contributed to rising tensions in Europe. When war broke out in 1914, the United States declared its neutrality. After Germany's ruthless march through neutral Belgium, however, American sympathies were almost entirely with the Anglo-French allies, though most still wanted to stay out of the war. That changed when Germany decided to initiate unrestricted submarine warfare.

At root submarine warfare in the twentieth century was simply a more technologically advanced form of commerce raiding. In its objective it resembled both privateering during the American Revolution and the voyages of the CSS *Alabama* and other raiders during the Civil War. Yet somehow striking unarmed merchant ships from the depths, often without warning, seemed particularly heinous. Just as the use of underwater mines in the Civil War had horrified contemporaries before their use became routine, the employment of submarines against merchant shipping shocked public sentiment in the early months of World War I. When a German U-boat torpedoed and sank the British passenger liner *Lusitania* in May 1915, with the loss of nearly 1,200 lives, including 128 Americans, Americans were outraged. Germany insisted that the *Lusitania* was a legitimate target because it was carrying munitions, but the German government nevertheless offered assurances that such a thing would not happen again. Yet only eight months later, in February 1917, Germany announced a resumption of unrestricted submarine warfare aimed at starving Britain into submission. Nine weeks after that, on April 6, the United States declared war against Germany.

The months between the sinking of the *Lusitania* and the American declaration of war witnessed the only full-scale battleship fleet engagement in history. For most of the war the huge and expensive British and German battle fleets remained quietly in port on opposite sides of the North Sea, but in May 1916 the German fleet sortied. The ensuing confrontation, the Battle of Jutland (May 31–June 1, 1916), involved fifty battleships plus several hundred other warships. The Germans got the best of it, which was a shock to Britons, who were used to hearing of Royal Navy triumphs. In the end, however, it made little strategic difference, for afterward the German fleet returned to its base at Kiel, and the two fleets never fought again.

Two months after the Battle of Jutland, the U.S. Congress voted for a historic expansion of the U.S. Navy by enacting what is sometimes called the Big Navy Act of 1916. President Woodrow Wilson supported the act not necessarily to prepare the country for war but to ensure that it could defend its Atlantic frontier regardless of who emerged triumphant in Europe. The new bill authorized ten dreadnought battleships, six battlecruisers (armed like battleships but with less armor), ten "scout cruisers," fifty destroyers, and, interestingly, sixty-seven submarines. The new battleships were to be enormous. Whereas the original *Maine* had displaced 6,300 tons and the *Indiana* class battleships displaced 10,000 tons, four of the new American dreadnoughts would displace 42,000 tons, and they would carry 16-inch guns, the largest guns yet placed on a warship.

None of these vessels had been completed when the United States declared war on Germany in April 1917, and almost immediately it became obvious that the greatest peril to the Allied cause at sea was not Germany's battleships but her U-boats. By then the German U-boats were sinking Allied ships faster than they could be replaced. The United States therefore halted construction of the big battleships and battlecruisers and devoted the men and material thus saved to building an armada of destroyers for escort duty.

Thanks in part to Rear Admiral William S. Sims, sent to London just before the war began, the Anglo-American allies established a system of convoys in which destroyers and other small armed warships escorted merchant vessels through the danger zone off England and Ireland. Navy men had initially resisted the idea of convoys. Herding slow and balky merchant ships was passive and reactive, and convoy duty itself was tedious and unglamorous. In the end, however, convoys proved essential to Allied victory at sea.

Meanwhile, as the ground war staggered on to its bloody conclusion on the western front, the American dreadnoughts

On the Same Team

Enlist in the WAVES

APPLY TO YOUR NEAREST
NAVY RECRUITING STATION OR OFFICE OF NAVAL OFFICER PROCUREMENT

6. A 1942 recruiting poster directly solicits women volunteers for what was called "Women Accepted for Volunteer Emergency Service" or WAVES. Though the designation as "emergency" volunteers ended at the end of World War II, women remained a part of the naval service into the post-war era.

authorized in 1916 remained unfinished—steel skeletons awaiting completion. The United States did send a division of older coal-burning pre-dreadnoughts to join the British fleet at Scapa Flow, north of Scotland, more as a gesture of solidarity than a genuine contribution to Allied naval power.

The U.S. Navy also helped to erect a minefield across the northern exit from the North Sea to keep German U-boats from getting into the Atlantic sea lanes. By the end of the war the Americans had sown more than fifty-six thousand mines and the British another sixteen thousand. Although this may have deterred some U-boats, there is little evidence that it had a significant impact on the war effort.

Like all wars, World War I also triggered social change. A famous U.S. Navy recruiting poster of 1917 portrayed a comely young woman in a sailor suit exclaiming, "Gee I Wish I Were a Man, I'd Join the Navy." Soon enough she could. Women had served as nurses in the navy since 1908; the first twenty of them came to be known as "the sacred twenty" since they were the first women to serve in uniform. During World War I their number grew to more than 1,500, though all of them served in hospitals ashore rather than on shipboard. In addition Secretary of the Navy Josephus Daniels announced that the navy would also begin to accept females as yeomen, a naval rating that designated secretarial duties, and before the war was over some 11,000 women served in this role. A year later the U.S. Marine Corps accepted the first women marines; they worked as accountants, typists, and stenographers. Despite these modest reforms, sea service and combat duty remained the exclusive province of males.

The treaty navy

The Great War ended on November 11, 1918, a date still celebrated, particularly in Britain, as Armistice Day. The ensuing negotiations at Versailles outside Paris produced a treaty that mandated German reparations to the Allies and established a League of Nations. The League had been the special project of President Wilson, who attended the peace conference in person. Yet upon his return to the United States, Wilson was unable to convince either the American public or, more significant, the U.S. Senate of the wisdom of participation in the League, and the treaty failed ratification. In an anticlimactic denouement, Congress marked the end of American participation by simply repealing its declaration of war. Congress preferred to protect U.S. interests by relying on national resources rather than on an international organization. In that spirit Congress decided to resume work on the still unfinished battleships of the 1916 authorization.

It was not clear who the presumed opponent for this expanded battleship navy might be. The German High Seas Fleet no longer existed. As part of the armistice agreement, the Germans had interred their battleship fleet at the British naval base at Scapa Flow, and once it became evident that the British planned to claim those ships as part of German reparations, their German crews scuttled them. That made the Royal Navy the only possible opponent for an enlarged U.S. battle fleet, and given the cordial relations and close cooperation that had existed between the Royal Navy and the U.S. Navy during the war, that was all but unthinkable. Yet because the British were committed to maintaining the world's largest navy, it was evident that if the United States continued with its 1916 program, the British would feel obligated to respond with a renewed building program of their own. The consequence might well be another expensive arms race, this time between allies, and for no reason beyond inertia and tradition.

Motivated by such considerations, the Warren G. Harding administration that took office in 1921 proposed that a naval arms conference should be held in Washington, D.C., that fall. At the very first session of this conference the U.S. secretary of state,

Charles Evans Hughes, laid out an audacious proposal: that the major navies of the world should reduce their arsenal of battleships by sinking or scrapping a significant number of them. The United States was prepared to scrap twenty-eight of its own battleships, he declared, including many of the brand-new dreadnoughts, and other nations would be expected to sacrifice as well. Once all these ships had been destroyed, Hughes told the delegates, each nation would retain enough battleships to establish a stable ratio among the great powers. Despite subsequent haggling about particular ships and special exemptions, the basic outline of Hughes's proposal was eventually embedded in the Washington Naval Arms Limitation Treaty of 1922. The shorthand reference for the battleship ratio thus established was 5:5:3, the numbers representing the relative battleship strength of the United States, Britain, and Japan. The treaty was very specific in defining battleships as any vessel that displaced over 10,000 tons and carried guns larger than eight inches. For that reason, after 1922 a number of nations built ships that slipped just under these limits and were universally known as "treaty cruisers."

One noteworthy consequence of the 1922 treaty was its impact on the development of aircraft carriers, a warship type so new that only experimental versions existed when the treaty was signed. The treaty put limits on carriers as well as battleships, yet the totals allocated to each power (135,000 tons for the United States and Britain; 81,000 tons for Japan) left plenty of room for continued experimentation and growth. Moreover the treaty specifically authorized the signatory powers to convert unfinished battleship and battlecruiser hulls into carriers. Up to then carriers had been relatively small, and the few planes they carried were used primarily to scout for the battleships or to observe the fall of shot from the ships' big guns. Adapting the much larger hulls of battleships or battlecruisers for use as aircraft carriers made those ships capable of carrying sixty to eighty planes or more, which transformed them from scouts for the fleet into offensive platforms in their own right. In the U.S. Navy this led to the commissioning of the carriers *Lexington* and *Saratoga* in 1928, each of which displaced more than 40,000 tons and carried as many as eighty aircraft.

A second naval arms limitation conference took place in London in 1930 in an effort to apply the 5:5:3 formula to cruisers. The new treaty limited the United States to eighteen heavy cruisers, with Britain allowed fifteen and Japan twelve. The agreement was valid for only five years, however, and in the mid-1930s Japan declined to renew it. At about the same time Adolf Hitler renounced the restrictions of the Versailles Treaty on Germany's navy.

The interwar navy

There was retrenchment of another kind in the post–World War I years concerning the navy's enlisted force. The reduction in the size of the navy meant that it could no longer accept all who wished to serve, a circumstance exacerbated by the economic depression that dominated the 1930s. The number of women nurses dropped from 1,550 to thirty-two, and African Americans in the navy found their opportunities severely restricted until nearly all of them served as stewards, or what were known as "mess boys." The same was true of Filipino enlistees, who were able to join the U.S. Navy after the Philippines achieved Commonwealth status in 1935 but were largely restricted to service as stewards. All officers were white men who were served meals by stewards who were black or brown. Women in the navy all but disappeared.

Despite the cutbacks, the fleet continued to conduct its annual exercises, and navy planners both in Washington and at the Naval War College continued to develop contingency plans, each of which was identified by a color that indicated the potential foe. There were more than two dozen of these plans for potential wars against almost every possible enemy, including Britain, Germany, France, and Mexico. There was even a War Plan Indigo for a possible occupation of Iceland. The plan that dominated the navy's strategic thinking, however, was Plan Orange for a war against Japan.

The central element of Plan Orange was the assumption that the Japanese would attempt to seize the Philippines. When they did, American army forces there would defend a fortified position in the Bataan peninsula near Manila for up to six months while an American battle fleet mobilized in Hawaii for a showdown with the Japanese fleet somewhere in the Philippine Sea. Though Mahan had died in 1914, his shadow continued to influence American naval planners, who fully expected that a future war in the Pacific would be decided by a Jutland-like confrontation between opposing lines of dreadnoughts.

In March 1933 Franklin D. Roosevelt took the oath of office as president. Roosevelt's highest priority was dealing with the effects of the ongoing economic depression, but like his distant cousin Teddy (who was also his uncle by marriage), he was a lifelong navy enthusiast who had read Mahan as a child and had served as assistant secretary of the navy. The navy he inherited as president had fallen to its lowest levels since 1902. With only eleven battleships in service, the U.S. Navy had not even managed to maintain the strength allotted to it by the 1922 treaty. Then, in 1934, Japan announced its intention to repudiate the 1922 treaty altogether, and a year later Hitler in Germany disavowed the disarmament clauses of the Versailles Treaty and began to rearm. Alarmed by these developments, Roosevelt threw his support behind a naval expansion program. The Vinson-Trammell Act of 1934 authorized an eight-year program to bring the navy up to the limits authorized by the 1922 treaty, and another act in 1938 enlarged the navy by an additional 20 percent. Given prevailing antiwar sentiments, that was as far as public opinion would allow him to go.

Then, in September 1939, Germany invaded Poland and World War II began.

Chapter 8

The two-ocean navy: the U.S. Navy in World War II (1939–1945)

Europe went back to war in 1939 with more dread than enthusiasm. It had been barely twenty years since "the war to end all wars," and the horrifying memories of trench warfare were still fresh for many. Hitler's revitalized Wehrmacht rolled over Poland in a matter of weeks, then turned west to confront Anglo-French forces along the Maginot Line. After a winter's lull—the so-called Phony War—the Germans began their western offensive in May 1940. Using an effective combination of quickly moving armored columns paired with tactical air strikes—a new form of warfare called *blitzkrieg*—the Germans sliced through Belgium into France, drove the British Expeditionary Force to the beaches at Dunkirk, and forced the French to request an armistice. On June 22 France capitulated.

One month later, on July 19, the U.S. Congress passed the Two-Ocean Navy Act, the largest naval appropriation in American history. It expanded the U.S. Navy by more than 70 percent, authorizing 257 warships, including eighteen aircraft carriers, seven battleships, thirty-three cruisers, 115 destroyers, and forty-three submarines, plus fifteen thousand combat aircraft. None of these ships, however, would be available for many months, if not years, and in the meantime the crisis deepened.

The undeclared naval war

Though the United States remained officially neutral in the European War, President Franklin Roosevelt did not ask the American people to be impartial. Instead he openly supported the British, determined that the United States should provide whatever Britain needed to prevent a collapse. For the next year and a half, as Britain withstood the Blitz and fought a rear-guard action in North Africa, Roosevelt tested the political and legal boundaries of neutrality, going as far as public opinion would allow to provide tangible support to the beleaguered United Kingdom.

As in World War I, what Britain needed most was more escorts to protect the convoys that constituted her lifeline to the world. The United States had more than a hundred idle World War I-era destroyers laid up in the nation's navy yards. Roosevelt would have been happy simply to give them away, but isolationists and an economyminded Congress insisted on a quid pro quo. In September 1940 FDR negotiated a deal whereby Britain turned over several valuable naval bases to the United States, most of them in the Caribbean, in exchange for fifty old destroyers. The arrangement satisfied Congress that the president had struck a pretty good bargain—which he had.

The most important program Roosevelt instituted to aid the British was Lend Lease, which allowed the United States to provide Britain with the tools of war—even weapons and munitions—with the understanding that the British would return them afterward. Roosevelt characterized this as lending a garden hose to a neighbor whose house was on fire, overlooking the fact that it was unlikely that any of the "hoses" would ever be returned. Roosevelt hoped that by providing this support, the Nazis could be defeated without the United States having to become an active belligerent.

In June 1941 British victory seemed far away as German armies drove deep into Russia and her U-boats savaged the Atlantic convoys. To protect those convoys and the Lend Lease equipment they carried, Roosevelt authorized U.S. Navy ships to patrol the western Atlantic, to cooperate with the Royal Navy, and even to convoy merchant ships as far as Iceland. The imperious and exacting commander of the U.S. Atlantic Fleet, Admiral Ernest J. King, put U.S. warships on a wartime footing, and soon enough confrontations between American destroyers and German U-boats escalated into a virtual undeclared naval war. In September 1941 a U-boat fired a torpedo at the USS *Greer* but missed; in October a U-boat torpedo struck the USS *Kearney*, killing eleven American sailors and wounding twenty-two others; a few weeks after that a U-boat actually sank the USS *Reuben James*, killing 115 Americans. These actions might have led to open war, but both sides stepped back: Hitler because he was fully extended in Russia, and Roosevelt because of fierce opposition from isolationists at home.

Meanwhile Roosevelt was also negotiating with the Japanese, who had embarked on their own campaign of conquest in Asia. In the hope that it might act as a restraint on Japanese behavior, Roosevelt ordered that the Pacific battle fleet be relocated from the west coast of the United States to Pearl Harbor in Hawaii.

The Pacific, 1941–1943

On December 7, 1941, planes from six aircraft carriers of the Imperial Japanese Navy struck the U.S. fleet at Pearl Harbor. The Japanese had concluded that in order to complete their conquest of South Asia, they needed to clear the way by eliminating the U.S. battleship fleet. The Pearl Harbor attack unified the American people and galvanized them for war. Four days later Hitler too declared war on the United States, plunging the United States into a two-ocean war in partnership with Great Britain, though the British conceded management of the Pacific war to the Americans early on. The Soviet Union was not quite a full partner in this war. Because the Russians were engaged in a furious death struggle with Germany along a thousand-mile front, they did not declare war on Japan.

The first six months of the war in the Pacific did not go well for the Americans. There were a few moments of satisfaction, such as when the carrier *Hornet* transported sixteen U.S. Army bombers under the command of Colonel Jimmy Doolittle to a launching position six hundred miles off mainland Japan for a raid on Tokyo and other cities in April 1942. For the most part, however, the Japanese had everything their way, compiling a long string of victories that included the capture of the British citadel of Singapore in February and the American-held Philippines in April. The Japanese carrier force even raided into the Indian Ocean, raising Allied fears of a Japanese-German linkup in the Arabian Sea and the Persian Gulf.

The rampage by the Japanese carrier force, along with the American attack on Tokyo, signaled that the aircraft carrier had replaced the battleship as the primary weapon of naval warfare. That was confirmed in May 1942, when American and Japanese carrier forces fought to a tactical draw in the Battle of the Coral Sea northeast of Australia. It was the first naval battle in history where the opposing forces never sighted one another.

The idea of flying airplanes off ships dated back to the dawn of aviation itself. In 1910, only seven years after the Wright brothers conducted the first heavier-than-air flight, a civilian pilot named Eugene Ely flew a Curtiss biplane off a ramp built on the cruiser USS *Birmingham*, and a year later Ely landed an aircraft on the battleship *Pennsylvania*. When the United States entered World War I, the navy had fifty-four aircraft and forty-eight aviators, including student aviators, though all of them flew from shore bases. In 1922 the U.S. Navy erected a flight deck on the hull of the old collier *Jupiter*, which, rechristened the *Langley*, became the navy's first aircraft carrier. Soon afterward the carriers *Lexington* and *Saratoga* were constructed using two unfinished battlecruiser hulls in conformance with the Washington Treaty. Almost nine hundred feet long and displacing more than 40,000 tons, they were so large as to transform their function. Instead of acting as support ships for the fleet, they became the spearhead of a strike force.

The turning point of the Pacific war came on June 4–5, 1942, with the stunning American victory in the Battle of Midway. The Americans were greatly aided in this engagement by a group of dedicated code-breakers, who were able to glean just enough information from decrypted Japanese naval messages to allow Admiral Chester Nimitz to pre-position his three carriers north of Midway Atoll, from which point they ambushed the Japanese as they approached. In the ensuing confrontation air groups from the U.S. carriers sank all four of the Japanese carriers, while losing only one of their own. The recorded radio message traffic during the battle reflects the almost giddy mood of the American dive bomber pilots who achieved this improbable victory:

> "That scared the hell out of me. I thought we weren't going to pull out."
> "Your bomb really hit them on the fantail. Boy that's swell."
> "Look at that son-of-a-bitch burn."
> "Those Japs are as easy as hitting ducks in a rain barrel."
> "Gee, I wish I had just one more bomb."
> "Tojo, you son-of-a-bitch, send out the rest and we'll get them, too."

It was one of the most decisive and strategically important naval battles in history. Though the war had more than three full years to run, after Midway the Japanese largely conceded the initiative to the Americans.

Only a month later, in August 1942, the United States took the offensive in the Pacific, landing a division of U.S. Marines on the

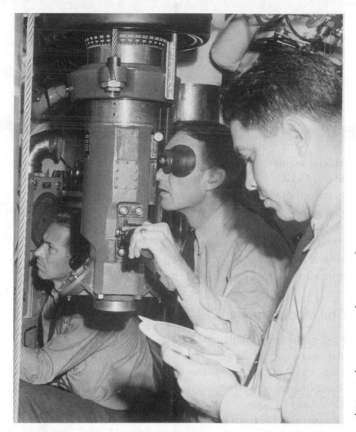

7. A U.S. Navy officer in the Pacific peers through the periscope of a submarine in 1942. American submarines accounted for 55 percent of all Japanese ship losses in the Pacific theater of World War II and cut Japan off from essential imports, especially oil.

island of Guadalcanal in the Solomon Islands, northeast of Australia. The Japanese counterattacked, and the result was a series of naval battles in and around the Solomon Islands from August 1942 to February 1943. So many ships were lost—on both sides—that the body of water north of the Guadalcanal beachhead came to be known as Iron Bottom Sound. Though the Japanese won a number of tactical successes in these battles, none was decisive, and their collective losses severely eroded their assets, especially the loss of trained naval aviators.

Worse was to come. Though the U.S. Navy had possessed submarines since the early twentieth century, they came fully into their own during the war in the Pacific. The first operational order issued to the fleet after Pearl Harbor was to "execute unrestricted air and submarine warfare against Japan." Given that the United States had declared war on Germany in 1917 ostensibly for its use of unrestricted submarine warfare, it was a measure of how the culture and values of warfare had evolved that the country employed this form of warfare without hesitation or anguish. Though American torpedoes proved unreliable during the first several months of the war, by 1943 American submarines were wreaking havoc on Japanese shipping.

The Mediterranean, 1943–1944

Well before the United States entered the war in December 1941, American and British policymakers had agreed that if and when the United States became an active belligerent, the English-speaking partners should concentrate on defeating Germany first because it was by far the strongest and most dangerous of the three Axis powers—Germany, Italy, and Japan. Josef Stalin, whose forces were bearing the brunt of the European war, repeatedly called for the Anglo-American Allies to open a second front by invading German-occupied France, but in 1942 the Allies simply did not have the assets to do so.

In addition, at the beginning of 1942 the German U-boats were still winning what was called the Battle of the Atlantic, the two-year struggle of Allied convoys and their escorts with German U-boats often operating in groups called wolf packs. In this duel each side sought to intercept and decode the other's radio message traffic either to locate the convoys or to avoid the wolf packs. The German goal was to sink Allied ships faster than American construction yards could build them. By the end of 1942, though the Atlantic remained a dangerous place, the Allies were winning that race.

U.S. Army Chief of Staff George C. Marshall wanted to focus Allied energies on building up forces in England for a cross-Channel attack in 1943. Roosevelt, sensitive to the impatience of the public and the sacrifices of the Russian armies, did not want to wait until then to strike. The result was a decision to invade French North Africa in the fall of 1942.

Dubbed Operation TORCH, the Anglo-American invasion of Morocco and Algeria initiated an extended Allied campaign in the Mediterranean. The Anglo-Americans finally drove the Germans from the African continent in May 1943 and soon afterward invaded Sicily and then Italy. Allied task forces, with Rear Admiral H. Kent Hewitt commanding the American force, escorted the transports to the target beaches, carried the men and their equipment ashore, and provided close-in naval gunfire support. Hewitt's task force of more than five hundred ships included not only cruisers and destroyers but also specially designed amphibious ships like the Landing Ship Tank (LST) and Landing Craft Infantry (LCI). The invasion of Italy knocked the Italians out of the war, but it also delayed by a year the cross-Channel invasion into northern France, which Allied planners now scheduled for May 1944.

Meanwhile the unprecedented demand for more ships, more planes, and more manpower contributed to social change at home, and in particular opened new opportunities for women. In addition to "Rosie the Riveter" in airplane factories and "Wendy the Welder" in shipyards, women were welcomed into the military services in unprecedented numbers. In the army women joined the WAACs (Women's Auxiliary Army Corps), and in the navy they enlisted in the WAVES (Women Accepted for Volunteer Emergency Service).

Once again most of the work the WAVES did was clerical, and they did not serve aboard warships, but they freed up thousands of men for sea service by doing essential support work ashore. Moreover, despite the designation as "emergency" service, it proved difficult to reinstate male exclusivity after the war, and in 1948 the WAVES became part of the regular U.S. Navy.

The Central Pacific drive, 1943–1944

Even as British and American soldiers fought their way across Africa and up the Italian boot, the United States effectively abandoned the Germany-first strategy by launching twin offensives in the Pacific. That the United States could sustain simultaneous campaigns on opposite sides of the world was a testament to the nation's unprecedented industrial output. By late 1942 the first products of the Two-Ocean Navy Act of 1940 began to join the fleet. Whereas in June 1942, the United States had been hard-pressed to assemble three aircraft carriers for the Battle of Midway, a year later twenty-four new *Essex*-class aircraft carriers joined the fleet, each of them displacing more than 30,000 tons and carrying ninety to one hundred aircraft. Soon afterward nine more *Independence*-class carriers joined the fleet. These thirty-three carriers, along with ten new fast battleships (so called because their speed of 28 to 30 knots allowed them to keep pace with the swift carriers), constituted a striking force more powerful than the entire navy of any other country in the world.

U.S. shipyards also turned out an unprecedented number of cruisers, destroyers, and destroyer escorts, plus more than 2,700 Liberty Ships—the essential transport and cargo vessels of the war—as well as thousands of specialized landing ships essential to amphibious operations. In 1943 alone American shipyards turned out more than eight hundred of the large LSTs and LCIs, plus more than eight *thousand* of the smaller landing craft known as Higgins boats, after their designer Andrew Jackson Higgins. With this unprecedented naval strength, the United States prepared to fight its way across the Pacific to the very shores of Japan and to conduct a landing in Nazi-occupied France.

One curious and occasionally awkward characteristic of the Pacific campaign was the division of authority between Army General Douglas MacArthur, who headed the Southwest Pacific Theater that included Australia and the Philippines, and Admiral Chester Nimitz, who commanded the Pacific Ocean Area that included everything else from Hawaii to Japan. MacArthur's forces conducted a campaign northward from Australia and westward along the north coast of New Guinea, while Nimitz's forces, spearheaded by the powerful fleet of new carriers and fast battleships, initiated the Central Pacific Drive: an island-hopping campaign that began at the tiny island of Tarawa in the Gilbert Islands in November 1943.

8. New P-47 Thunderbolt fighters crowd the flight deck of the escort carrier USS *Casablanca* in mid-1944. The production of hundreds of new ships and thousands of new planes during World War II made the U.S. Navy the most powerful sea force ever created.

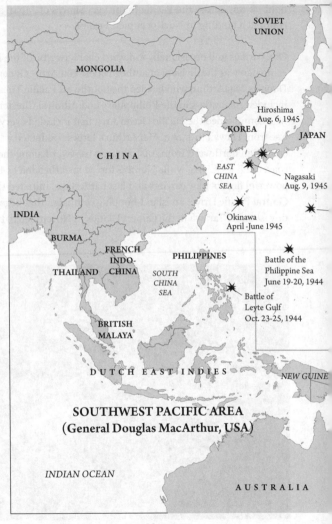

SOVIET
UNION

MONGOLIA

Hiroshima
Aug. 6, 1945

KOREA

JAPAN

CHINA

*EAST
CHINA
SEA*

Nagasaki
Aug. 9, 1945

INDIA

Okinawa
April-June 1945

BURMA

FRENCH
INDO-
CHINA

PHILIPPINES

THAILAND

*SOUTH
CHINA
SEA*

Battle of the
Philippine Sea
June 19-20, 1944

BRITISH
MALAYA

Battle of
Leyte Gulf
Oct. 23-25, 1944

DUTCH EAST INDIES

NEW GUINE

SOUTHWEST PACIFIC AREA
(General Douglas MacArthur, USA)

INDIAN OCEAN

AUSTRALIA

9. The Pacific theater in World War II.

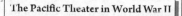

PACIFIC OCEAN

Battle of
Midway
June 4-6, 1942 ✳ *MIDWAY*

Iwo Jima
Feb. 19 - March 26, 1945

HAWAII

Pearl Harbor ✳
Dec. 7, 1941

PACIFIC OCEAN AREA
(Admiral Chester Nimitz, USN)

✳ Landings on Kwajalein
Jan. 31 - Feb.3, 1944

✳ Landings on Tarawa
Nov. 20-23, 1943

Naval Battles of Guadalcanal
✳✳ Aug. 1942-Feb. 1943

Battle of the Coral Sea
May 7-8, 1942

SAMOA

FIJI

*NEW
CALEDONIA*

| 0 | 500 | 1000 Miles |
| 0 | 500 | 1000 Kilometers |

The Tarawa invasion was a sobering wake-up call for the U.S. Navy and Marines. Tiny as it was, Tarawa was defended by five thousand crack Japanese soldiers, and before the three-day battle was over, only seventeen of them were taken alive. The U.S. Marines suffered three thousand casualties. Similar ferocious resistance met the Navy–Marine Corps team in other landings from Kwajalein in the Marshall Islands to Saipan in the Marianas, and eventually at both Iwo Jima and Okinawa. American losses were heavy, but Japanese losses were heavier due mainly to near absolute American supremacy at sea and in the air. Only twice did Japan attempt to regain control of the seas around the targeted islands by sending out its main battle fleet. Each of these efforts triggered a major naval battle.

The first of them took place on June 19–20, 1944, in the Philippine Sea west of Saipan, when the Japanese sent out their fleet in the hope of destroying the American covering force under Admiral Raymond Spruance. The Japanese committed nine carriers to the fight, plus several battleships and cruisers. But the Americans had fifteen carriers and more than nine hundred planes, twice as many as the Japanese. The result was a daylong air battle in which navy pilots from the American carriers shot down 315 Japanese airplanes while losing only thirty of their own. Far worse for the Japanese was the fact that they also lost all but a very few of the pilots of those 315 planes, while most of the American pilots were recovered. A shortage of trained carrier pilots would hamstring Japanese operations for the rest of the war. The Americans later dubbed this fight "the Great Marianas Turkey Shoot."

The second attempt by the Japanese to interfere with an American landing resulted in the Battle of Leyte Gulf (October 23–25, 1944), the largest naval engagement in history. On October 21, U.S. soldiers returned to the Philippines, landing in the sheltered waters of Leyte Gulf. The American Seventh Fleet under Vice Admiral Thomas Kinkaid, part of MacArthur's command, covered the approaches to the beachhead from the south, while the U.S.

Third Fleet under Vice Admiral William F. "Bull" Halsey, part of Nimitz's command, covered approaches from the north. The divided U.S. command structure invited confusion in American communications.

The Japanese used their remaining carriers (now mostly bereft of planes and pilots) as bait in an effort to draw off Halsey's force. Eager to finish off the Japanese carriers, Halsey first crippled the approaching Japanese surface force with an airstrike, then turned north to get the enemy carriers. That uncovered the American beachhead in Leyte Gulf, and the Japanese surface force that Halsey had wounded turned around and headed toward the exposed American transports and landing ships. A handful of American destroyers and small escort carriers fought desperately, putting up a bold front, and at the last minute the Japanese turned away.

Despite this near disaster, the Battle of Leyte Gulf was an overwhelming American victory that destroyed the offensive potential of the Imperial Japanese Navy. American Rear Admiral Jesse Oldendorf's veteran battleships smashed up a Japanese surface force in Surigao Strait south of Leyte, and Halsey's carrier planes virtually annihilated the Japanese carriers off Cape Engaño to the north.

D-Day

While the American "Big Blue Fleet" fought its way across the Pacific, the Anglo-American Allies completed preparations for the long-delayed amphibious landing in northern France, dubbed Operation OVERLORD. The essential cooperation necessary to effect this huge and complex operation was greatly aided by the political sensitivity and deft management skills of the overall Allied commander, the American General Dwight D. Eisenhower. The naval element of OVERLORD was codenamed Operation NEPTUNE, and the Allied naval

commander was British Admiral Bertram Ramsay. Rear
Admiral Alan G. Kirk commanded the American task force
under Ramsay, and Rear Admirals Don P. Moon and John
Lesslie Hall commanded the naval forces for the American
beaches codenamed Utah and Omaha.

The first and in many ways the greatest challenge faced by the
Allies in executing this plan was the daunting logistical
difficulty of transporting the soldiers, their equipment, and their
supplies, and then sustaining the invaders during the critical
buildup. In that effort the bottleneck was a shortage of LSTs, the
large tank and troop carriers used in every Allied landing from
Italy to the Philippines. Nevertheless on June 6, 1944, the first
elements of the Allied invasion force landed on five target
beaches in Normandy in northern France. The landings on
Omaha Beach in particular were touch and go, and the close-in
fire support of a handful of U.S. and Royal Navy destroyers
proved critical, but despite heavy losses, by the end of the day
the Allies had secured a toehold. The commander of the
American First Army, General Omar Bradley, acknowledged
in his report, "The Navy saved our hides."

As important as the initial landings were, the continuous
buildup over the next two months was equally critical. In the
three weeks after D-Day, Allied landing ships and transports
put more than 300,000 men, fifty thousand vehicles, and
150,000 tons of supplies ashore on Omaha Beach alone. By
the first week of July the Allies had more than a million fully
equipped soldiers ashore ready to break out of their enclave
in Normandy and Brittany for a campaign to Paris and
eventually Berlin.

In August the Allies landed in southern France. Hewitt, now a vice
admiral, commanded the naval forces that put two divisions of the
U.S. Seventh Army and the First French Army ashore. Unlike in
Normandy, Axis resistance in southern France was weak, and the

Allies quickly drove inland, heading northward up the Rhone Valley as the Allied forces in the north raced toward Paris, which fell on August 25.

Iwo Jima, Okinawa, and the end of the war

Iwo Jima is a small volcanic island in the Bonin Island chain about halfway between Saipan and the home islands of Japan. Its military value was that it could provide a base for American fighters to escort the long-range bombers from Saipan to and from Japan and provide an emergency landing field for the bombers. To secure it U.S. Marines landed on Iwo Jima's black sand beach on February 19, 1945, and the ensuing month-long campaign cost them 6,800 killed and more than twenty thousand wounded. It was a terrible price to pay for an emergency airfield. The ferocity of the fighting is suggested by the fact that of the twenty-one thousand Japanese defenders, only 216 were taken alive.

Okinawa is the largest of the Ryukyu Islands and the last stepping-stone before the invasion of the home islands. To defend it the Japanese employed that most desperate of weapons, the kamikazes—airplanes stuffed with explosives and flown by volunteers willing to sacrifice their lives by crashing into American ships. Altogether the Japanese sent more than 1,500 kamikazes to hurl themselves at the American fleet around Okinawa. American pilots and anti-air gunners shot down most of these, but those that got through sank thirty-six U.S. ships and crippled 368 others, losses so severe that at one point the U.S. high command considered calling off the operation. Nevertheless the landings went forward, and after a campaign of nearly three months and American casualties of nearly forty thousand killed and wounded, Okinawa fell.

By now Japan was virtually defenseless. American planes bombed Japanese cities at will, and American submarines had isolated the home islands from the rest of the world, cutting off her access to oil. By the summer of 1945 Japan had few assets left. Yet the concept of surrender was so alien to Japanese culture that without some kind of near mystical intervention, there seemed to be no option to a war of annihilation. The mystical intervention came in the shape of a mushroom cloud as U.S. Air Force bombers dropped atomic bombs on Hiroshima on August 6, 1945, and on Nagasaki on August 9. That same day the Soviet Union declared war on Japan.

With Germany having capitulated in May, the formal surrender of the Japanese on the deck of the American battleship *Missouri* on September 2, 1945, brought World War II to an end. The two-ocean war had propelled the U.S. Navy to a new position as the dominant naval power on earth.

Chapter 9
Confronting the Soviets: the Cold War navy (1945–1975)

The sine wave that traced the periodic increase and contraction of the U.S. Navy reached an unprecedented apogee in the fall of 1945. Having entered World War II with eleven active battleships and seven aircraft carriers, the U.S. Navy ended the war with 120 battleships and cruisers and nearly one hundred aircraft carriers (including escort carriers). Counting the smaller landing craft, the U.S. Navy listed an astonishing sixty-five thousand vessels on its register of warships and had more than four million men and women in uniform. It was more than twice as large as all the rest of the navies of the world combined.

The sine curve did ease downward after 1945. In the eighteen months after the end of the war, the navy processed out 3.5 million officers and enlisted personnel who returned to civilian life and their families, going back to work or attending college on the new G.I. Bill. In addition thousands of ships were scrapped or mothballed, assigned to what was designated as the National Defense Reserve Fleet and tied up in long rows at navy yards from California to Virginia. Though the navy boasted only about a thousand ships on active service by the end of 1946, that was still more than twice as many as before the war. The contraction was less draconian than after previous wars because of the almost immediate emergence of what has come to be called the Cold War: a forty-year period of tension and rivalry between the

United States and the Soviet Union. Though the two superpowers never actually fought one another, they did participate in a number of hot wars through surrogates. The fact that, after 1949, both sides possessed nuclear weapons raised the stakes in this rivalry to a chilling dimension.

Defense unification and deterrence

Despite near universal recognition that unified command was essential to military success, the United States had continued to operate throughout World War II under a bureaucratic system in which the War and Navy Departments were separate branches of government. That archaic system was finally changed in 1947 with passage of the National Defense Act, which created a Department of Defense, with the army, navy, and the newly created air force all subordinate elements of a unified command system. That did not end the squabbling among the services for resources, however, and the most disruptive of these squabbles erupted in 1949, when Secretary of Defense Louis Johnson decided to halt the construction of the navy's new 60,000-ton aircraft carrier, prospectively named the *United States*, and use the money to build a fleet of new long-range bombers for the air force: the B-36.

Johnson's decision alarmed the navy leadership, for the *United States* had been designed to accommodate aircraft that could carry nuclear weapons, which would give the navy a role in strategic deterrence. The cancellation of the *United States* therefore appeared to be not merely a choice between weapons systems but a decision to make the air force primarily responsible for deterring Soviet aggression in the nuclear era. The vice chief of naval operations, Admiral Arthur Radford, testified before Congress that the B-36 was a "billion dollar blunder," and when Chief of Naval Operations Louis Denfeld endorsed Radford's criticism, Johnson dismissed him. This episode, dubbed "the Revolt of the Admirals," created a political firestorm. After a lengthy investigation Congress criticized the manner of Denfeld's dismissal (though not the decision itself) and added a new supercarrier to the next year's defense budget. That ensured the navy a role in strategic deterrence.

Within a decade the navy's deterrent mission was greatly enlarged by the construction of a new class of nuclear-powered, missile-firing submarines (SSBNs), colloquially called "boomers." These remarkable boats (submarines are generally called *boats* rather than *ships*) were possible due in large part to the fierce commitment of Rear Admiral (later Vice Admiral) Hyman G. Rickover, who not only supervised the design and construction of the first nuclear-powered submarine, the USS *Nautilus*, in 1955 but also made nuclear submarines a kind of personal fiefdom. The *Nautilus* was an attack submarine, which meant that, like its conventional predecessors, its primary weapon was the torpedo. Then, in late 1959, the United States produced the first submarine that could fire a Polaris missile while submerged, the USS *George Washington*. The *Nautilus* could sink a ship, but the *George Washington* could incinerate a city. During the next eight years a total of forty-one such submarines joined the navy's arsenal.

Over the ensuing quarter century American ballistic missile submarines became larger, faster, and quieter. In 1981 the United States launched the first *Ohio*-class submarine, which was more than three times the size of the *George Washington*. The missiles too became larger, with a longer range and with multiple, independently targetable warheads. In 1972 the Poseidon missile replaced the Polaris, and in 1979 the Trident replaced the Poseidon. The boomers remained almost continually at sea; to do that they had two crews, a Blue crew and a Gold crew, that swapped places after each cruise. These men (and they were all men until 2011) remained submerged for months at a time, sleeping in bunks between the missile tubes and living in a fully self-sustained artificial environment.

By the late 1970s the United States had come to rely on a so-called triad of deterrence platforms: land-based bombers and land-based intercontinental ballistic missiles (ICBMs), both under the supervision of the air force, and the navy's fleet of SSBNs. While deterring a Soviet missile strike remained the primary mission of all of America's services throughout the Cold War, the United States also confronted a series of smaller wars around the world.

The Korean War

Among the several geographical oddities that resulted from the end of World War II was the division of Korea along the 38th parallel. Initially that demarcation was no more than an administrative convenience to denote where either Russian or American units would accept the surrender of the occupying Japanese. As in Europe, however, once the Red Army moved into an area, it showed a stubborn unwillingness to depart, and by 1949 the two halves of Korea had become, in effect, separate countries.

On June 25, 1950, the Soviet-supplied army of North Korea crossed the 38th parallel in the first overt military aggression of the Cold War era. Facing weak opposition, the North Koreans quickly drove southward, pinning South Korean forces and their outnumbered American allies into a defensive toehold around the port city of Pusan. President Harry S. Truman successfully organized support from the United Nations, which had been chartered in 1945 to replace the ineffective League of Nations, but it was clear from the start that the United States would take the lead in repelling this aggression. U.S. Navy forces, including a task force built around the carrier USS *Valley Forge*, struck at the North Korean supply lines, but the most effective response would be an amphibious landing behind North Korean lines. General Douglas MacArthur argued for a landing at Inchon, the seaport for the South Korean capital of Seoul. Though most senior officers feared that a landing at Inchon was too risky due to the narrow ship channel into the harbor and thirty-foot tides, MacArthur's ebullient confidence carried the day.

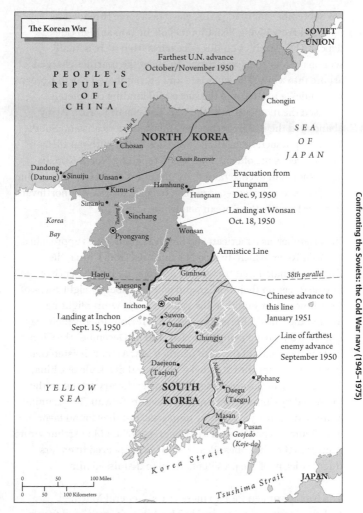

The Korean War

PEOPLE'S REPUBLIC OF CHINA

SOVIET UNION

Farthest U.N. advance October/November 1950

Chongjin

SEA OF JAPAN

NORTH KOREA

Yalu R.

Chosan

Chosin Reservoir

Dandong (Datung)
Sinuiju
Unsan
Kunu-ri
Hamhung
Hungnam

Evacuation from Hungnam Dec. 9, 1950

Sinanju
Taedong R.
Sinchang

Landing at Wonsan Oct. 18, 1950

Korea Bay

Pyongyang

Imjin R.

Wonsan

Armistice Line

Haeju
Kaesong
Gimhwa

38th parallel

Inchon
Seoul
Suwon
Osan

Chinese advance to this line January 1951

Landing at Inchon Sept. 15, 1950

Chungju

Han R.

Cheonan

Line of farthest enemy advance September 1950

Daejeon (Taejon)

Nakdong R.

Pohang

YELLOW SEA

SOUTH KOREA

Daegu (Taegu)

Masan
Pusan
Geojedo (Koje-do)

Korea Strait

Tsushima Strait

JAPAN

| 0 | 50 | 100 Miles |
| 0 | 50 | 100 Kilometers |

Confronting the Soviets: the Cold War navy (1945–1975)

10. The Korean War

On September 15, 1950, a U.S. Navy task force threaded its way up the narrow Flying Fish Channel off Inchon at high tide to deposit U.S. Marines on three "beaches" that were actually sections of an urban waterfront. In effect the marines charged ashore into a city. The surprised and outnumbered North Koreans were quickly routed, and the successful landing completely reversed the momentum of the war. The North Korean Army abandoned the Pusan perimeter, and the Americans and South Koreans pursued them all the way back to the 38th parallel. Within weeks the official objective of repelling North Korean aggression had been achieved. At this point, however, MacArthur sought—and received—permission to continue the war northward in order to unify the Korean peninsula.

In November, as American and South Korean forces approached the Yalu River, which divided North Korea from China, the Chinese signaled that they would not tolerate the presence of hostile forces on their border, and on November 27 eight corps of the Chinese Army crossed the Yalu. In fierce winter fighting around the Chosin Reservoir, the U.S. Marines fought their way southward to avoid being encircled, and by December the Chinese had pushed south of the 38th parallel. MacArthur insisted that the war must now be extended with a naval blockade of China, the bombing of Chinese cities, and a diversionary attack on the mainland by Chinese Nationalist forces on Taiwan. The Truman administration rejected these proposals, but they found favor with Truman's political foes in Congress. When MacArthur wrote a letter to the Republican leadership that appeared to endorse their criticism of the president, Truman dismissed him.

The war continued for two more years. General Matthew Ridgway assumed command in MacArthur's stead, and forces under his command gradually fought their way back to the vicinity of the 38th parallel. In July 1953 the two sides signed an armistice that made the cease-fire line a de facto boundary, as it remains today.

The Korean War ended in a stalemate, yet American forces, supported by troops from South Korea and other United Nations members, succeeded in repelling the first cross-border invasion by communist forces during the Cold War. That encouraged American lawmakers to continue support of a robust peacetime navy, and of military forces generally. Whereas U.S. military spending in 1950 had totaled $141 billion, for the rest of the 1950s it averaged over $350 billion per year.

The Middle East

The overall architecture of American and Soviet rivalry influenced, and even defined, virtually every aspect of American foreign and defense policy in the Cold War years. Even when the issue at hand had little to do with the Soviet Union, every political and military dispute from 1949 onward was likely to be viewed through the prism of how it affected the East-West balance of power. This was particularly true in Europe, where Germany was divided into rival occupation zones and where the United States sponsored the establishment of the North Atlantic Treaty Organization (NATO) to present a common front to deter Soviet aggression.

It was also true in the Middle East, which in the immediate postwar years was destabilized by two circumstances. The first was the establishment in 1948 of the Jewish state of Israel in the former British mandate of Palestine, a decision that bred resentment among both the Palestinians and their Arab neighbors. The United States strongly backed the creation of the state of Israel and applauded the 1948 Israeli victory over the combined forces of Egypt, Jordan, and Syria when those nations banded together in an effort to eliminate it. The other issue that defined Middle East politics and diplomacy was the West's continued reliance on oil from the Persian Gulf region. Though the United States was less dependent on Middle East oil than either Britain or Japan, it maintained a policy of ensuring access for its allies.

In 1950 the United States established a permanent naval presence in the Mediterranean—the Sixth Fleet—generally composed of one or two aircraft carriers plus a dozen or so cruisers and destroyers. Throughout the Cold War years it constituted the strongest naval force in the region. Early on, however, it became evident that having the biggest fleet did not result in the ability to control events, especially within the complex environment of the Middle East.

In 1956 Egypt's president Gamal Abdel Nasser decided to nationalize the French- and British-owned Suez Canal. When British, French, and Israeli forces orchestrated a coordinated attack on Egypt to reclaim the canal for their investors, it was not clear what, if anything, the United States should do about it. Under the direction of President Dwight Eisenhower, U.S. Navy Chief of Naval Operations Arleigh Burke directed Vice Admiral Charles R. Brown, then commanding the Sixth Fleet, to "prepare for imminent hostilities." Brown's reply underscored the uncertainty of his situation: "Am prepared for imminent hostilities, but which side are we on?" Eventually a UN resolution supported by the United States called on all sides to withdraw, and Egypt assumed control of the canal in 1958.

That same year Lebanon's president, Kamil Shamun, requested American support to suppress unrest in Beirut. U.S. Marines landed on Beirut's beaches south of the city amid surprised and amused holiday tourists, but this comic opera beginning nearly led to hostilities between the Americans and the Lebanese Army, which resented the intrusion. In the end cooler heads prevailed, though the event demonstrated once again that naval power was not a magic wand that could resolve all complex issues.

This was evident as well during the so-called Six Day War in June 1967 between Israel and her Arab neighbors, Egypt, Syria, and Jordan. The United States was again supportive when Israel's superbly trained army easily won the land war. In the midst of the fighting, however, Israeli air forces attacked a U.S. Navy intelligence-gathering vessel, the USS *Liberty*, in the Mediterranean, killing thirty-four Americans and wounding 171 others. Despite suspicions, then and later, that the Israelis had targeted the *Liberty* deliberately in order to protect the security of their military communications, the Lyndon Johnson administration readily accepted a subsequent Israeli explanation of mistaken identity, mainly because the United States did not want to create a rift with Israel.

The Cuban Missile Crisis, 1962

The use of naval power proved more effective closer to home. In the early fall of 1962 the Soviet Union placed intermediate-range nuclear missiles in Cuba. Informed of the buildup, President John F. Kennedy determined to stop it by imposing what he called a "naval quarantine"—essentially a blockade—of Cuba. His decision was a middle ground between those of his advisers who argued for an air attack to destroy the missiles and those who argued for opening negotiations. There was substantial risk in choosing a blockade strategy, for it created the possibility—even the likelihood—that U.S. and Soviet ships would confront one another face-to-face. In addition, while a blockade might prevent more missiles from coming into Cuba, it could not remove the missiles that were already there. Still, Kennedy believed it provided the right combination of forcefulness and restraint.

For thirteen days the world all but held its collective breath as the crisis played itself out. On October 27 a Soviet vessel, the *Groznyy*, refused to obey the order of an American destroyer to stop and be inspected. After several tense hours the American destroyer fired several warning shots past the *Groznyy*, which finally caused her to stop. Eventually the Soviet ship reversed course and retreated to the quarantine line. In the end the Soviets agreed to remove their missiles from Cuba.

A noteworthy aspect of this crisis was the extent to which navy ships were able to remain in continuous communication not only with the task force commanders but also with policymakers. In the nineteenth century captains at sea had been all but sovereign, making decisions not only as ship commanders but also as virtual policymakers. Now, in an age of swift radio communications, the president of the United States could personally monitor the individual twists and turns of a destroyer engaged in a delicate confrontation with a potential enemy.

The Vietnam War, 1965–1974

The dominance of the Cold War paradigm over most U.S. policy decisions also contributed to America's star-crossed involvement in Vietnam. Though President Kennedy had sent thousands of military advisers to the pro-Western government of South Vietnam to aid in its fight with communist insurgents, it was an incident at sea that triggered active U.S. participation. In August 1964 two U.S. Navy destroyers operating off communist North Vietnam in the Tonkin Gulf reported that they had been attacked by North Vietnamese PT boats. A few nights later the captain of the USS *Maddox* reported a second attack. Though there is some uncertainty whether the second attack occurred at all, President Johnson asked Congress to give him broad powers to protect American security interests in the area. On August 10 Congress quickly and overwhelmingly approved what became known as the Gulf of Tonkin Resolution.

The war thus begun eventually lasted nine years and cost more than 210,000 American casualties, including 58,209 killed. In that war the U.S. Navy had three primary missions: carriers operating on Yankee Station in the Gulf of Tonkin launched air strikes against targets in North Vietnam; navy ships along the South Vietnamese coast sought to interdict communist supply routes; and small U.S. Navy gunboats, both armored and unarmored, patrolled the labyrinth of waterways known collectively as the Mekong Delta.

In all these efforts the ambiguities of fighting in the midst of a civil war in a distant country with a harsh climate and unfamiliar culture frustrated American operators. Pilots of strike aircraft found that the rules of engagement severely restricted their freedom of action in selecting targets. Then too the loss of even a few U.S. planes on these missions often put their pilots into the hands of the North Vietnamese government, and that gave the North Vietnamese disproportionate leverage in subsequent peace negotiations.

U.S. Navy skippers charged with patrolling the South Vietnamese coast in what was dubbed Operation MARKET TIME found it all but impossible to tell friend from foe among the hundreds of wooden junks and sampans. Much of the inshore work was conducted by eighty-four small (fifty-foot) patrol craft officially dubbed PCFs (patrol craft, fast) but which everyone called Swift Boats. Divided into five coastal squadrons, they patrolled the lengthy coast of South Vietnam from the 17th parallel to Cape Camau in the Gulf of Thailand. Stopping scores of small fishing vessels every day was both frustrating and dispiriting and also bred resentment among those who were searched.

The third navy theater of operations during the Vietnam War was in the treacherous Mekong Delta. In this flat and featureless plain of some fifteen thousand square miles, the southward-flowing Mekong River breaks into four outlets connected by scores of canals and small waterways. The Vietnamese communists (Viet Cong or VC in the American parlance) used the marshy swamps and thick foliage of the Delta as a sanctuary. To disrupt those sanctuaries and to interdict enemy communications, the U.S. Navy initiated Operation GAME WARDEN. As off the coast, the navy relied on scores of small, light, fiberglass-hulled vessels called PBRs (patrol boat, river), which spent most of their time stopping and searching suspicious vessels. Often their suspicions were justified. From 1966 to 1968 the PBR sailors of Operation GAME WARDEN engaged in an average of more than two firefights a day. For heavier action the navy used specially modified landing craft that were heavily armored, and which were dubbed "monitors" in a tribute to Ericsson's Civil War innovation. Despite constant patrols and frequent engagements, the U.S. Navy never quite succeeded in eliminating the Viet Cong threat from the Delta.

All in all, though the U.S. Navy's nine-year experience in Vietnam was marked by many examples of individual heroism and sacrifice, it was also frustrating and often dispiriting. The war ended not on the battlefield but at a conference table. The Paris Peace Accords of January 1973 guaranteed the right of South Vietnam to choose its own government, though in fact the North Vietnamese and their allies inside South Vietnam toppled that government almost immediately, and by 1975 Vietnam had become a unified and communist country.

U.S. Navy culture

The years of war in Vietnam were also marked by social upheavals at home. Opposition to the war, limited at first but stronger as the war lengthened, was part of a new cultural dynamic. America fractured over the war, with older citizens generally supporting it while younger citizens opposed it. Protests were ubiquitous on college campuses, and they eventually led to violence, most notably at Kent State University in May 1970, when National Guard forces killed four students and wounded nine. At the same time, the United States was also roiled by the impact of the civil rights movement. President Johnson had signed the 1964 Civil Rights Act less than a month before the Tonkin Gulf incident, and over the ensuing decade protests against the war and protests for civil rights often became blurred.

These social currents affected the U.S. Navy as well. On one level there was a divide between older service members, especially the chief petty officers, who tended to be traditionalists, and younger servicemen, including the junior officers, who welcomed change. Like the nation at large, the navy had serious racial issues. Black servicemen were often given menial jobs and were disproportionately subjected to nonjudicial punishment called Captain's Mast. In 1971 more than a hundred black sailors on the aircraft carrier USS *Kitty Hawk* held a protest meeting that blew up into a full-fledged race riot. A year later, on board the USS *Constellation*, fifty or so black sailors staged a sit-in strike on the mess decks.

It was partly in recognition of these problems that President Richard Nixon appointed Admiral Elmo "Bud" Zumwalt as chief of naval operations. Zumwalt had served effectively as the commander of naval forces in Vietnam, but his place in history derives largely from his service as CNO (1970–74). In that capacity he issued more than a hundred "Z-grams," messages addressed to all navy personnel that virtually transformed the institution. Some of these addressed weighty issues such as racial discrimination (Z-gram 66, issued in December 1970) and opportunities for women (Z-gram 116, issued in August 1972). Others dealt with more mundane subjects, such as allowing sailors to grow sideburns and mustaches, or establishing a more liberal liberty policy. As a result Zumwalt became a lightning rod for disagreements between traditionalists and reformers in the U.S. Navy of the late twentieth century. His reforms stood, however, and even the traditionalists came to accept them as essential, especially after Nixon abolished the draft in 1973, creating the all-volunteer military.

The Cold War was not over. U.S. Navy planners continued to base their assessments, their budget requests, and their force structure on a possible confrontation with the Soviet Union. But significant and historic changes were taking place in Moscow too.

Chapter 10
The U.S. Navy in the twenty-first century

Throughout the Cold War era the United States confronted the reality that great military power did not translate into the ability to control events. This was especially evident in 1979, when a mob of protestors in Iran, angered by U.S. support for the deposed shah, seized the U.S. embassy in Tehran and held fifty-two Americans hostage for more than a year. An outraged American public turned President Jimmy Carter out of office and sent Ronald Reagan to Washington in 1981. As a parting slap at Carter, who had welcomed the shah to the United States for medical treatment, the Iranian hostage-takers released their prisoners on the very day that Reagan was inaugurated.

Reagan had campaigned on a promise to reassert American greatness, and one of his earliest initiatives was to inaugurate a naval buildup with an announced goal of creating a six-hundred-ship navy. Reagan began that program not in response to a particular threat but as a kind of public reaffirmation of America's global leadership, and in that respect, it was similar to the aspirations of the navalists during the Age of Sail or Theodore Roosevelt's support for the Great White Fleet.

Though fiscal realities soon scuttled the idea of building or maintaining a six-hundred-ship navy, one aspect of the buildup was the reactivation of four *Iowa*-class battleships that had been completed toward the end of World War II. All four had been mothballed in 1956–58, after the Korean conflict, though one of them, the USS *New Jersey*, had been called back into service in 1968 for the Vietnam War before being decommissioned again a year later. In 1981 all four of them were reactivated and updated with new and sophisticated electronics as well as both Harpoon and Tomahawk missile launchers. Their visual impact made them impressive on the world stage and gave the United States four more battle groups that could be sent to trouble spots, but they were expensive to operate and not cost-effective as either gun platforms or missile launchers. In 1991–92 they were decommissioned for the final time. That marked the end of the Age of the Battleship, which had lasted almost exactly one hundred years. America's first modern battleship, the USS *Indiana* (BB-1), had been laid down in 1891, and its last, the USS *Missouri* (BB-63), was decommissioned in 1992.

Though Mahan had insisted that a nation's battleship fleet constituted an accurate gauge of its power and influence, it had become evident by the middle of World War II that battleships had been supplanted by aircraft carriers, which in the Cold War era grew increasingly large. The USS *Gerald R. Ford* (CVN-78), commissioned in 2013, displaces 110,000 tons, eleven times that of the USS *Indiana*. Even before the end of the twentieth century, some critics were beginning to wonder if the country was putting too many of its eggs into too few baskets.

The end of the Cold War

The Cold War came to an abrupt end in the late 1980s. Westerners had long noted that despite its robust military, the Soviet Union struggled economically to maintain its global position, and very likely the effort to keep pace with increased American military spending taxed the Soviet economy even more. Still, when the end came, it caught nearly everyone by surprise. In 1982 the top-secret National Intelligence Estimate concluded, "We believe this [Soviet] wartime strategy will remain essentially unchanged over the next 15 to 20 years." Yet nine years later the Soviet Union itself no longer existed.

For forty years the United States and the U.S. Navy had centered all of its attention on the rivalry with the Soviet Union. All planning for defense budgets, for force structure, and for the design of weapons systems grew out of assessments of the Soviet threat. The dissolution of the Soviet Union therefore compelled navy planners to revisit almost all of their assumptions. It did not erase the need for a global U.S. Navy, for even as the Soviet Union was collapsing, events in the Middle East and elsewhere provoked serial crises that led to the dispatch of U.S. naval combat groups to a variety of hot spots around the world. On the other hand, these new threats were so different from those of the Cold War era that the sophisticated weaponry the United States had developed to deter and, if necessary, defeat the Soviet Union did not necessarily meet the needs of what President George H. W. Bush called "a new world order."

The wars in Iraq and Afghanistan

The Iranian hostage crisis of 1979–80 left lingering animosity between the United States and Iran, and when Iraq invaded Iran in September 1980, though the United States remained officially neutral, it "tilted" (as one U.S. State Department official put it) toward Iraq, providing several billion dollars' worth of aid to Saddam Hussein's government. The Iran-Iraq war dragged on for eight years even as the Soviet Union collapsed and the Cold War came to an end. By then the war in the Persian Gulf had become the third bloodiest conflict of the twentieth century, with well over a million dead. Though the United States was not a participant in the war, it was a measure of its emerging role as global umpire that it took on the task of escorting neutral tankers through the war zone.

It was dangerous work. On April 14, 1988, the guided-missile frigate USS *Samuel B. Roberts* struck a mine that had been placed in the main shipping channel by the Iranian Revolutionary Guard, and President Reagan authorized a retaliation. In a measured reprisal codenamed PRAYING MANTIS three U.S. Navy Surface Action Groups destroyed several Iranian gas and oil separation platforms in the Gulf. The Iranian Navy ventured out of port in response, and that triggered the largest surface naval engagement since World War II. On April 18, 1988, U.S. Navy forces sank two Iranian warships and badly damaged a third. Significantly they did so using surface-to-surface missiles rather than gunfire, though one Iranian vessel was sunk by aircraft from the carrier USS *Enterprise*.

Once again technology had enlarged the battlefield. In the Age of Sail combatants fought one another from a range of fifty to a hundred yards; during the Spanish-American War navy gunners fired from two miles away; and in World War II pilots flying from carriers targeted ships a hundred miles away. Now missiles could be fired from either surface ships or submarines at targets well beyond the horizon. That did not reduce the danger, for the use of advanced technology was not limited to the U.S. Navy. During the engagement in the Persian Gulf, sailors on the USS *Wainwright* recalled hearing "this big whoosh going down the starboard side from forward to aft" as a U.S.-made Harpoon missile, fired from the Iranian patrol boat *Joshan*, flew past so close that the men on the *Wainwright* could smell the propellant.

As it turned out, the action in April 1988 marked only the beginning of American military and naval operations in the Persian Gulf. Though the United States had backed Saddam's war against Iran, when he invaded the small country of Kuwait in August 1990, President Bush declared, "This will not stand," and organized an international coalition to drive Iraqi forces out of Kuwait. The Gulf War of 1991 was a spectacular success that demonstrated both the impressive capability of a new generation of sophisticated electronic weapons as well as the post–Cold War role of the United States as world policeman.

A decade later, on September 11, 2001, terrorists under the direction of Saudi billionaire Osama bin Laden flew hijacked commercial airliners into the twin towers of the World Trade Center in New York and the Pentagon in Washington, causing nearly three thousand deaths. A fourth hijacked airplane, perhaps intended to destroy the U.S. Capitol building, crashed in the Pennsylvania countryside after the passengers rose up against the hijackers. Upon learning that bin Laden's terrorist organization, called al-Qaeda (the Base), had trained in Afghanistan, President George W. Bush authorized an attack on the anti-Western Taliban government there. As in Kuwait a decade earlier, the American war in Afghanistan was swift and successful, although establishing and maintaining a stable pro-Western government afterward proved elusive.

Less than two years after that, in March 2003, the United States embarked on a second war against Iraq. The official explanation and justification was that Saddam's government was developing "weapons of mass destruction," though that proved not to be the case. Once again America's suite of sophisticated weapons quickly overwhelmed the Iraqi Army, and this time U.S. forces did continue all the way to Baghdad to topple the regime. As in Afghanistan, however, establishing and maintaining a stable and democratic government there proved difficult, and the peacekeeping effort stretched out to an indefinite future.

The wars in Afghanistan and Iraq necessarily involved naval support, and much of the ground fighting was done by the navy's Marine Corps partners, yet neither can be properly considered a naval war, for Iraq's small navy posed little threat, and landlocked Afghanistan had no navy at all. The wars did, however, illuminate a new template of naval combat for the post–Cold War era. Once the U.S. Navy decimated the Iranian

Navy in April 1988, the greatest naval threat in the Persian Gulf came not from enemy surface vessels but from cheap, crude weapons such as the mine that damaged the USS *Samuel B. Roberts* in 1988 and the small rubber boat filled with explosives and manned by fanatical volunteers who blew themselves up alongside the USS *Cole* in Yemen in October 2000. While America's sophisticated Cold War weaponry easily overpowered its foes in both Iraq wars, it was evident that such weapons were not ideally suited for the kind of small-scale constabulary missions against terrorists and lawbreakers that constituted much of the navy's responsibility in the post–Cold War years.

Pirates and smugglers

Nearly two hundred years after the United States formed the West Indian Squadron to deal with Caribbean piracy in the 1820s, the U.S. Navy in the twenty-first century again found itself confronted with a piracy problem. The focus of much of it was off the coast of Somalia near the horn of Africa. The pirates operated in small boats that were towed out to sea by a diesel-powered mother ship. Armed mostly with machine guns and an occasional rocket-propelled grenade (RPG) launcher, the pirates seized unarmed tankers and container ships passing along the coast, then held the ships and their crews hostage.

To combat this menace the U.S. Navy created Task Force 150, part of the navy's Central Command headquartered in Bahrain. In 2002 this became an international force, Combined Task Force 150, that included the ships of six other nations as well as those of the United States. U.S. Navy ships patrolled the coast as a deterrent force and occasionally participated in gun battles with armed pirates. As one example, on March 18, 2006, the USS *Gonzalez* observed a diesel trawler towing two small boats, the characteristic pattern of piracy operations. When the *Gonzalez* and the USS *Cape St. George* sent small inflatable boats to investigate, the Somalis opened fire and drove them off.

Remarkably the alleged pirates then pursued the inflatables and opened fire on the two U.S. Navy warships with RPGs and .50 caliber machine guns. The navy ships returned fire, destroying the pirate mother ship and capturing the two small gunboats. The captured pirates insisted they were only defending themselves and were eventually returned to their homeland in Somalia.

Another mission of the U.S. Navy reminiscent of its earlier duties in the Age of Sail was the interdiction of smugglers. Smuggling drugs into the United States from Mexico and Central America became endemic in the latter decades of the twentieth century. Off the coast of California and in the Gulf of Mexico as well as off the horn of Africa, shore-based U.S. Navy P-3 surveillance aircraft directed U.S. Navy and Coast Guard vessels, often carrying special operations teams, to intercept suspected drug smugglers as well as human traffickers.

In many of these operations a key component was the U.S. Navy's sea, air, and land teams, known as SEALs. These special operations forces trace their origins back to the amphibious scouts who conducted clandestine reconnaissance during World War II, such as the Navy Combat and Demolition Units (NCDUs) that went ashore on the Normandy beaches in advance of the D-Day landings in 1944 and the Underwater Demolition Teams (UDTs) that operated in the Pacific. SEALs received their modern name during the Vietnam War, and since then they have operated, mostly in great secrecy, in a wide variety of locations and circumstances.

Navy culture

The enlisted force of the U.S. Navy in the twenty-first century is largely a reflection of the nation at large. African Americans have served in the U.S. Navy since its founding, and because of that the navy was less affected than the other services by President

Truman's July 1948 order desegregating the military. Nevertheless that order, as well as the civil rights revolution of the 1960s and 1970s, significantly broadened opportunities for black Americans in all the services. In 2014 nearly 20 percent of U.S. Navy personnel self-identified as black or African American, a larger percentage than in the nation as a whole (12.6). Blacks are represented in the highest ranks as well, and 10 percent of the navy's admirals (sixteen of 160) are black. Sailors who self-identify as Hispanic or Latino/Latina make up about 15 percent of the navy's enlisted force, which very nearly matches their percentage in the country at large (16), though only four of the 160 active-duty admirals are Hispanic.

Eighteen percent of the navy's enlisted force and 17 percent of its officers are women. An important milestone in gender equality was the decision in 1976 to admit women to all three of the service academies, including the Naval Academy, which graduated its first women in 1980. Even then women were not eligible for combat roles, though one female member of the Naval Academy class of 1981, Wendy Lawrence, became both a jet pilot and an astronaut. In 1993 women began serving on combat vessels, though still not in dedicated combat roles. Despite that, women pilots flew missions over Iraq to enforce a no-fly zone after the first Gulf War, and they performed in a variety of combat assignments in the second Gulf War, including firing Tomahawk missiles into Iraq. One stubborn barrier to women serving in the U.S. Navy was their restriction from the submarine service. That barrier fell in November 2011, when the first class of women to complete nuclear power school reported aboard two "boomers" and two nuclear attack submarines. Three years later three women passed the rigorous program required of U.S. Marine Corps combat officers.

Another important change in U.S. Navy culture concerned the right of gay and lesbian Americans to serve openly. Until the late twentieth century homosexuality was a crime in all branches of the American military. Sodomy was a specific violation of the Uniform Code of Military Justice (UCMJ), punishable by a court-martial, and even absent any homosexual activity simply being gay was grounds for a less than honorable discharge. Growing understanding of homosexuality led to the establishment of a new policy in 1994 in which gays and lesbians could serve in the military so long as they remained closeted—a policy that came to be known as "Don't ask, don't tell." Under those rules gay and lesbian sailors and marines could serve unless their sexual orientation became known, at which point they would be dismissed. This awkward policy was abolished in 2011, after which all services, including the U.S. Navy, accepted gay and lesbian service members without qualification.

The U.S. Navy today

The official roster of U.S. Navy warships in 2014 listed 283 "battle force ships" on active service. While that is fewer than at any time since World War I, those ships possess more capability and firepower than the rest of the world's navies combined. American naval dominance in the twenty-first century is due in part to the absence of rivals. The quiet contraction of the Royal Navy after 1945 and the implosion of the Soviet Union in 1991 removed the nearest competitors to U.S. naval supremacy. Of course history does not stand still, and there are rising powers in the world. China in particular may pose a future challenge, though the current gap between the U.S. and Chinese navies is enormous. China's navy, rather awkwardly called the People's Liberation Army Navy, began to emerge from its historic role as a coastal force at the end of the twentieth century. In 2012 China commissioned its first aircraft carrier, and two more are in the planning stage, with delivery scheduled for 2020. That may or may not signal a Chinese ambition to challenge the United States for naval supremacy in the western Pacific. For the present, however, as well as for the foreseeable future, the U.S. Navy remains supreme on the oceans of the world.

Like the country it serves, the navy has evolved through several stages in its nearly 250 years. Part of that evolution is technological, as steamships replaced frigates, carriers replaced battleships, and missile platforms replaced gun turrets. That evolution continues. The completion of a number of so-called stealth ships, such as the high-speed USS *Zumwalt*, commissioned in 2014, gives the modern U.S. Navy increased electronic invisibility, and the technological leap from the American destroyers that served in World War II to the *Zumwalt* is as great as the one from Old Ironsides to the *Monitor*.

Another aspect of the navy's evolution over the past two and a half centuries is cultural. The largely illiterate international crews that manned U.S. Navy ships in the Age of Sail and that were kept in line by the carrot of a daily grog ration and the stick of the cat-of-nine-tails gave way to a mostly native-born enlisted force that reflects the heterogeneous character of the population. Moreover that enlisted force is rigorously trained in specialized schools ashore, and their graduates fulfill a wide variety of responsibilities as, among other ratings, aviation machinists mates, electronic technicians, and information systems technicians. The officer corps too has undergone change both demographically and culturally. No longer the exclusive province of well-connected gentlemen, it is populated by men and women of every race and religion.

Finally, an understanding of the evolution of the U.S. Navy requires an appreciation of the dramatic transformation of America itself, and especially its role in the world. In the Age of Sail the ambition of American policymakers was to avoid overseas entanglements. In the age of steam and steel the United States began to look outward, and in the later years of the nineteenth century the country embraced a Pacific empire. The twentieth century—the American century—saw the nation, and its navy, emerge to assume the status of global prominence, if not preeminence.

11. The guided missile destroyer USS *Zumwalt*, named for the nineteenth U.S. Chief of Naval Operations, has a startlingly different configuration from earlier warships. Her design is engineered to defeat unfriendly radar, making her a stealth warship.

In the twenty-first century the U.S. Navy continues to fulfill many of its historic missions: suppressing pirates, protecting trade, and pursuing drug runners. It is also a potent instrument of American foreign policy and a barometer of American concern; the arrival of an aircraft carrier battle group anywhere in the world is an unmistakable signal to friend and foe alike that the United States is paying attention. As President Bill Clinton said during a visit to the USS *Theodore Roosevelt* in 1993, "When word of a crisis breaks out in Washington, the first question that comes to everyone's lips is 'Where are the carriers?'"

In addition to its deterrent and peacekeeping roles, the U.S. Navy of the twenty-first century also acts as a first responder when typhoons, earthquakes, and other natural or man-made disasters call for humane intervention. Helicopters from the USS *Abraham Lincoln* were the first to arrive at stricken Banda Aceh in Indonesia after a tsunami there wiped out a whole city in December 2004, and a navy task force that included the hospital ship *Comfort* arrived in Haiti to assist the survivors of a devastating earthquake that killed more than 200,000 people there in January 2010. In that respect the U.S. Navy is the global cop on the beat: quelling pirates, chasing smugglers, deterring terrorists, and occasionally extending a humanitarian helping hand.

References

Chapter 2: Establishing an American navy

Quotations from the congressional debates and the ensuing legislation on the founding of the U.S. Navy are from *The Annals of Congress*, 42 vols. (Washington, D.C.: Gales & Seaton, 1834–56), 1:143, 154; and from *The Public Statutes at Large*, 86 vols. (Boston: Little, Brown, 1859–), 1:350, 621–22. Jefferson's reference to a "squadron of observation" is from Dudley Knox, ed., *Naval Documents Related to the United States Wars with the Barbary Powers*, 6 vols. (Washington, D.C.: U.S. Government Printing Office, 1939–44), 1:429.

Chapter 3: An American navy confirmed

Broke's note to Lawrence asking him "to try the fortune of our respective flags" is in William S. Dudley, ed., *The Naval War of 1812: A Documentary History* (Washington, D.C.: Naval Historical Center, 1992), 2:126.

The volunteer sailor who professed to be "in totle ignorance of the servis" was George Stockton, who wrote to Perry on September 5, 1813. The letter is in the Perry Papers, Clements Library, University of Michigan. The description of "mouldy" and "putrid" food is from Perry's report to Navy Secretary Jones of July 23, 1813, in "Letters Received by the Secretary of the Navy from Commanders, 1804–1886," National Archives, Record Group 45, microfilm reel 5. Commander's Letters, microfilm reel 5.

Perry's note to General Harrison is in Dudley, *The Naval War of 1812*, 2:553.

The Act for the General Increase of the Navy, specifying ships of "not less than 74 guns each," is from *Statutes at Large*, 3:321.

Chapter 4: A constabulary navy

The characterization of Mediterranean service as "a perpetual yachting party" is in Craig L. Symonds, *The Naval Institute Historical Atlas of the U.S. Navy* (Annapolis, MD: Naval Institute Press, 1995), 64.

The description of the Everglades as "a sea of mud" is from George Buker, *Swamp Sailors: Riverine Warfare in the Everglades* (Gainesville: University of Florida Press, 1975), 66.

Chapter 5: Steam and iron

The testimony of the *Virginia*'s engineer, E. A. Jack, is from *The Memoirs of E. A. Jack* (White Stone, VA: Brandywine, 1998), 14; and Craig L. Symonds, *Decision at Sea* (New York: Oxford University Press, 2005), 110.

Lincoln's observation that with the fall of Vicksburg, the Mississippi again flowed "unvexed to the sea" is from a letter Lincoln wrote to James Conkling on August 26, 1863, and is in Roy P. Basler, ed., *The Collected Works of Abraham Lincoln* (New Brunswick, NJ: Rutgers University Press, 1959), 6:409.

Chapter 6: The doldrums and the new navy

Oscar Wilde's short story "The Canterville Ghost" is discussed in John B. Hattendorf, ed., *The Papers of Stephen B. Luce* (Newport, RI: Naval War College Press, 1975), 1.

The passage from Secretary of the Navy B. F. Tracy's Annual Report is in U.S. Congress, *Annual Reports*, Secretary of the Navy, 1:45–50 and is discussed in Benjamin Franklin Cooling, *Gray Steel and Blue Water Navy* (Hamden, CT: Archon Books, 1979), 87–88.

Chapter 8: The two-ocean navy

The radio traffic during the Battle of Midway is from the Naval Records Service microfilm report on the Battle of Midway and is quoted in Symonds, *Decision at Sea*, 265–67. Bradley's comment

"The Navy saved our hides" is from his after action report and is
quoted in Craig L. Symonds, *NEPTUNE: The Allied Invasion of
Europe and the D-Day Landings* (New York: Oxford University
Press, 2014), 300.

Chapter 9: Confronting the Soviets

The characterization of the B-36 as a "billion dollar blunder" is from
Jeffrey G. Barlow, *Revolt of the Admirals: The Fight for Naval
Aviation, 1945–1950* (Washington, D.C.: Naval Historical Center,
1994), 222–33.
The messages between CNO Admiral Arleigh Burke and VADM
Charles R. Brown in 1956 are from Symonds, *The Naval Institute
Historical Atlas*, 200.

Chapter 10: The U.S. Navy in the twenty-first century

The prediction of an unchanged national security environment is from
the July 1982 National Intelligence Estimate, in Donald P. Steury,
ed., *Intentions and Capabilities: Estimates on Soviet Strategic
Forces, 1950–1983* (Washington, D.C.: Central Intelligence Agency,
1996), 476–81.
The memory of a "big whoosh going down the starboard side" comes
from an interview with Chief Petty Officer Reuben Vargas on
May 30, 2003, and is quoted in Symonds, *Decision at Sea*, 306.
President Clinton's remarks on board the USS *Theodore Roosevelt*,
March 12, 1993, are included in the American Presidency Project,
available at www.presidency.ucsb.edu.

Further reading

General

For more than half a century a standard reference for the history of the U.S. Navy has been E. B. Potter and Chester W. Nimitz, eds., *Sea Power* (Englewood Cliffs, NJ: Prentice-Hall, 1960), which was produced as a world naval history by a team of instructors at the U.S. Naval Academy for use in their classrooms. Twenty years later it was condensed into a shorter second edition with Potter as sole editor (Annapolis, MD: Naval Institute Press, 1981) that focuses on the U.S. Navy. A more detailed general history is by Robert W. Love Jr., *History of the U.S. Navy*, 2 vols. (Mechanicsburg, PA: Stackpole Books, 1993). Useful companions include James C. Bradford, ed., *Quarterdeck and Bridge* (Annapolis, MD: Naval Institute Press, 1997), which contains short biographies of many of the leading personalities of American naval history, from John Paul Jones to Elmo Zumwalt, and Kenneth Hagan, ed., *In Peace and War*, which is a collection of essays about the U.S. Navy from its birth to the present. Hagan's collection was initially published by Greenwood in 1978 but is available in a revised and updated edition (Westport, CT: Praeger, 2008). George Baer covers the years 1890–1990 in *One Hundred Years of Sea Power* (Stanford, CA: Stanford University Press, 1994). Two other books of special interest are Jack Sweetman, ed., *Chronology of the U.S. Navy and Marine Corps* (Annapolis, MD: Naval Institute Press, 1991), which is an indispensable reference, and Craig L. Symonds, *The Naval Institute Historical Atlas of the U.S. Navy* (Annapolis, MD: Naval Institute Press, 1995), which illustrates the events of U.S. naval history in 94 full-page color maps.

Chapter 1: An ad hoc navy

The principal source for naval activities in the American Revolution is *The Naval Documents of the American Revolution* (which has benefited from several editors), 11 volumes to date (Naval History Division, 1964–2005), which is available in an online version at ibiblio.org. A good general history of the American navy during the Revolution is William M. Fowler, *Rebels under Sail: The American Navy during the Revolution* (New York: Scribner, 1976). Administrative issues are the topic of Charles O. Paullin, *The Navy of the American Revolution* (Toronto: University of Toronto Press, 2011). James Nelson is the author of both *George Washington's Secret Navy* (Camden, ME: International Marine, 2008) and *Benedict Arnold's Navy* (Camden, ME: International Marine, 2006). Samuel Eliot Morison wrote a fine biography, *John Paul Jones* (Boston: Little, Brown, 1959), but see also Evan Thomas's biography, subtitled *Sailor, Hero, Father of the American Navy* (New York: Random House, 2010), which is a good read. Robert H. Patton discusses the business of privateering in *Patriot Pirates* (New York: Vantage, 2009), and the role of the French is in Jonathan R. Dull, *The French Navy and American Independence* (Princeton, NJ: Princeton University Press, 1975), though Barbara Tuchman's poignant *The First Salute* (New York: Random House, 1989) is not to be missed.

Chapter 2: Establishing an American navy

Books that analyze the congressional debates over the founding of the navy include George C. Daughan, *If By Sea: The Forging of the American Navy* (New York: Basic Books, 2008); Craig L. Symonds, *Navalists and Antinavalists: The Naval Policy Debate in the United States, 1785–1827* (Newark: University of Delaware Press, 1980); and Ian Toll, *Six Frigates: The Epic History of the Founding of the U.S. Navy* (New York: Norton, 2006).

The role of U.S. naval forces in the First Barbary War and the Quasi War are in two sets of collected documents, both edited by Dudley Knox: *Naval Documents Related to the United States Wars with the Barbary Powers*, 6 vols. (Washington, DC: Government Printing Office, 1939–44), and *Naval Documents Related to the Quasi-War*, 7 vols. (Washington, DC: Government Printing Office, 1935–38). Details on the specifications of U.S. Navy ships in the Age of Sail, including the gunboats, are in Howard I. Chapelle, *The History of the American Sailing Navy: The Ships and Their Development* (New York: Norton, 1949).

Chapter 3: An American navy confirmed

The newest and best book on British impressment of American sailors is Denver Brunsman, *The Evil Necessity: British Naval Impressment in the Eighteenth-Century Atlantic World* (Charlottesville: University of Virginia Press, 2013). Congressional debates over the declaration of war are in the *Annals of Congress*, 12th Congress, 1st session (the vote is on 2220). Official reports on naval actions in the War of 1812 are in William S. Dudley, ed., *The Naval War of 1812: A Documentary History*, 3 vols. (Washington, DC: Naval Historical Center, 1985–2002). On Rodgers's cruise see Charles O. Paullin, *Commodore John Rodgers* (Norman, OK: Arthur H. Clark, 1910). The frigate duels are described in a number of works, including Donald R. Hickey, *The War of 1812* (Champaign: University of Illinois Press, 1990), but see also the much older but still very readable Theodore Roosevelt, *The Naval War of 1812* (New York: Putnam's, 1899). On the Battle of Lake Erie, see John K. Mahon, "Oliver Hazard Perry, Savior of the Northwest," in James C. Bradford, *Quarterdeck and Bridge* (Annapolis, MD: Naval Institute Press, 1997), and Craig L. Symonds, *Decision at Sea* (New York: Oxford University Press, 2005), 23–79.

Chapter 4: A constabulary navy

On Perry and the African Squadron, see Samuel Eliot Morison, *"Old Bruin," Commodore Matthew C. Perry, 1794–1858* (Boston: Little, Brown, 1967), which is also the best source for Perry's mission to Japan, though see also John H. Schroeder, *Shaping a Maritime Empire: The Commercial and Diplomatic Role of the American Navy, 1829–1861* (Westport, CT: Praeger, 1985). On the Great United States Exploring Expedition, see Nathaniel Philbrick, *Sea of Glory* (New York: Penguin, 2004). Other USN exploring expeditions are chronicled in Vincent Ponko Jr., *Ships, Seas, and Scientists* (Annapolis, MD: Naval Institute Press, 1974). See also Steven J. Dick, *Sky and Ocean Joined: The U.S. Naval Observatory, 1830–2000* (Cambridge: Cambridge University Press, 2002), and on naval medicine in this era, see Harold D. Langley, *A History of Medicine in the Early U.S. Navy* (Baltimore: Johns Hopkins University Press, 2000). The best book on the Seminole War is John K. Mahon, *The Second Seminole War* (Gainesville: University Press of Florida, 1967). On the war with Mexico, see K. Jack Bauer, *The Mexican War, 1846–48* (Lincoln, NE: Bison Books, 1992), as well as Morison's *"Old Bruin."* The role of African American sailors is covered by W. Jeffrey Bolster in *Black Jacks: African American Seamen in the Age of Sail* (Cambridge, MA: Harvard University Press, 1998).

The officer corps in the Age of Sail is covered in depth by Christopher McKee in *A Gentlemanly and Honorable Profession: The Creation of the U.S. Naval Officer Corps, 1794–1815* (Annapolis, MD: Naval Institute Press, 1991), and the founding of the Naval Academy is covered in two recent books, one by William Leeman, *The Long Road to Annapolis: The Founding of the Naval Academy and the Emerging American Republic* (Chapel Hill: University of North Carolina Press, 2010), the other by Mark C. Hunter, *A Society of Gentlemen: Midshipmen at the Naval Academy, 1845–1861* (Annapolis, MD: Naval Institute Press, 2010).

Chapter 5: Steam and iron

The basic source for U.S. (and Confederate) Navy operations during the Civil War is the thirty-volume *Official Records of the Union and Confederate Navies in the War of the Rebellion* (Washington, DC: Government Printing Office, 1894–1922). Two secondary books that focus on the naval side of the conflict are James M. McPherson, *War on the Waters* (Chapel Hill: University of North Carolina Press, 2012), and Craig L. Symonds, *The Civil War at Sea* (New York: Oxford University Press, 2012).

An excellent discussion of the technological revolution of the 1850s is Kurt Hackemer, *The U.S. Navy and the Origins of the Military Industrial Complex* (Annapolis, MD: Naval Institute Press, 2001). Lincoln's management of naval forces is the subject of Craig L. Symonds, *Lincoln and His Admirals* (New York: Oxford University Press, 2008), while the role of the enlisted man is the subject of Michael Bennett in *Union Jacks* (Chapel Hill: University of North Carolina Press, 2004). William H. Roberts discusses Union ironclads in *Civil War Ironclads* (Baltimore: Johns Hopkins University Press,

2002), and William N. Still does the same for Confederate ironclads in *Iron Afloat* (Columbia: University of South Carolina Press, 1985). David Surdam covers economic issues in *Northern Naval Superiority and the Economics of the American Civil War* (Columbia: University of South Carolina Press, 2001).

Chapter 6: The doldrums and the new navy

Useful sources on the renaissance of the U.S. Navy are James L. Abrahamson, *America Arms for a New Century* (New York: Free Press, 1981), and Benjamin Franklin Cooling, *Gray Steel and Blue Water Navy* (Hamden, CT: Archon Books, 1979). Mahan's influential *The Influence of Sea Power Upon History* (Boston: Little, Brown, 1890) is available in several modern reprints. It is dominated by lengthy battle studies from the Age of Sail, but his introductory essay about the preconditions of sea power provides a summary of his argument. A useful general survey of the Spanish-American War is G. J. A. O'Toole, *The Spanish War: An American Epic, 1989* (New York: Norton, 1986), and Jim Leeke offers a brisk summary of the two principal naval battles in *Manila and Santiago: The New Steel Navy in the Spanish-American War* (Annapolis, MD: Naval Institute Press, 2009).

Chapter 7: A navy second to none

James Reckner wrote the standard book, *Teddy Roosevelt's Great White Fleet* (Annapolis, MD: Naval Institute Press, 2001). A detailed and readable account of the tangled tale of the Panama Canal is David McCullough's excellent *The Path between the Seas* (New York: Simon & Schuster, 1978). The story of HMS *Dreadnought* and the Anglo-German naval arms race is covered in detail in the first volume of Arthur Marder's classic work, *From Dreadnought to Scapa Flow* (New York: Oxford University Press, 1961). The U.S. Navy's activities during World War I are exhaustively covered in William N. Still Jr., *Crisis at Sea: The United States Navy in European Waters in World War I* (Gainesville: University Press of Florida, 2006).

Postwar naval policy is the subject of Harold and Margaret Sprout's *Toward a New Order of Sea Power* (Princeton, NJ: Princeton University Press, 1940), which is somewhat dated by their navalist enthusiasm. The Naval Arms Limitation Treaty is covered by Thomas

H. Buckley in *The United States and the Washington Conference, 1921-1922* (Knoxville: University of Tennessee Press, 1970).

Chapter 8: The two-ocean navy

The classic source for the study of the U.S. Navy during World War II is Samuel Eliot Morison's fifteen-volume semi-official *History of the United States Operations in World War II* (Boston: Little, Brown, 1947–62). A readable one-volume abridgment entitled *The Two-Ocean War* (Boston: Little, Brown, 1963) is available in a paperback edition published by the Naval Institute in 2007. Since Morison's wrote, scores of specialized studies, relying on newly uncovered material, have greatly expanded our knowledge of the navy's role in the war. Space prevents including all or even most of them, but among them are Gordon Prange's detailed study of the Japanese attack on Pearl Harbor, *At Dawn We Slept* (New York: McGraw-Hill, 1981); Walter Lord's study of Midway, *Incredible Victory* (New York: Harper & Row, 1967), as well as Craig L. Symonds, *The Battle of Midway* (New York: Oxford University Press, 2011); John Costello's *The Pacific War, 1941-1945* (New York: Rawson, Wade, 1981); James D. Hornfischer, *Neptune's Inferno: The U.S. Navy at Guadalcanal* (New York: Bantam, 2012), and Richard B. Frank, *Guadalcanal* (New York: Random House, 1990); Thomas J. Cutler, *The Battle of Leyte Gulf* (Annapolis, MD: Naval Institute Press, 1994). The U.S. Navy's five-star leaders are profiled by Walter R. Boneman in *The Admirals* (Boston: Little, Brown, 2012).

The Atlantic theater was dominated by the U-boat war. Michael Gannon covers the navy's fight against U-boats along the U.S. East Coast in *Operation Drumbeat* (Annapolis, MD: Naval Institute Press, 2009), and the Battle of the Atlantic is the subject of Ed Offey's *Turning the Tide* (New York: Basic Books, 2011). The naval side of the D-Day invasion is in Craig L. Symonds, *Neptune: The Allied Invasion of Europe and the D-Day Landings* (New York: Oxford University Press, 2014).

Chapter 9: Confronting the Soviets

The B-36 controversy is covered in depth by Jeffrey G. Barlow in *Revolt of the Admirals: The Fight for Naval Aviation* (Washington,

DC: Naval Historical Center, 1994). The opening phases of the Korean War are covered by Alan R. Millett in *The War for Korea, 1950–1951* (Lawrence: University Press of Kansas, 2010), but do not overlook the dated but still authoritative Robert D. Heinl, *Victory at High Tide: The Inchon-Seoul Campaign* (Mount Pleasant, SC: N&A Press, 1979). There are a number of books on the Cuban Missile Crisis. Among the best is Michael Dobbs, *One Minute to Midnight* (New York: Knopf, 2008). The navy's role in Vietnam is covered by Thomas J. Cutler in *Brown Water, Black Berets: Coastal and Riverine Warfare in Vietnam* (Annapolis, MD: Naval Institute Press, 1988). The controversial role played by Hyman Rickover in the development of the nuclear navy is covered by Norman Polmar and Thomas B. Allen in *Rickover: Father of the Nuclear Navy* (Lincoln, NE: Potomac Books, 2007). Another pivotal and controversial figure of this era is Elmo Zumwalt, who is presented sympathetically by Larry Berman in *Zumwalt* (New York: Harper, 2012), but see also Zumwalt's own memoir, *On Watch* (New York: New York Times Books, 1976).

Chapter 10: The U.S. Navy in the twenty-first century

Reagan's secretary of the navy, John Lehman, wrote a memoir about the naval buildup in the 1980s: *Command of the Seas* (New York: Scribner, 1988). Craig Symonds includes Operation PRAYING MANTIS, the 1988 surface action in the Persian Gulf, as one of the battles in *Decision at Sea: Five Naval Battles That Shaped American History* (New York: Oxford University Press, 2005), 265–320. Williamson Murray covers *The Iran-Iraq War* (Cambridge: Cambridge University Press, 2014); and Richard Lowry authored *The Gulf War Chronicles* (Bloomington, IN: iUniverse Star, 2008). The current status and strength of the world's navies are itemized in detail in *The Naval Institute Guide to Combat Fleets of the World*, 16th ed. (Annapolis, MD: Naval Institute Press, 2013). A more alarmist view of the U.S. Navy's current status in the world than the one presented herein is *Mayday: The Decline of American Naval Supremacy* by Seth Cropsey (New York: Overlook Press, 2014).

Index

Index